GOOD HOUSEKEEPING

STEP-BY-STEP

FOOD
PROCESSOR
COOKBOOK

GOOD HOUSEKEEPING

STEP-BY-STEP

FOOD
PROCESSOR
COOKBOOK

EBURY
PRESS

Ebury Press thank Moulinex for their assistance in the preparation
of this book. The food processors featured in the colour
photographs in the book and on the cover are from the Moulinex
range.

Published by Ebury Press
National Magazine House
72 Broadwick Street
London W1V 2BP

First impression 1984
Second impression 1985
Third impression 1985

ISBN 0 85223 387 6 (hardback)
0 85223 334 5 (paperback)

Designers: Bob Hook/Ivor Claydon
Photographer: Theo Bergstrom

Filmset by Advanced Filmsetters (Glasgow) Ltd

Printed by Hazell Watson and Viney Ltd.
Aylesbury

Contents

Introduction

If you have recently bought a food processor, you will soon be wondering how you ever managed without it. If you have owned one for some time it is doubtless already your firm friend, standing by at all times of the day to help you with the tedious and time-consuming jobs that have to be done to food—before it gets into the oven or on to the table. If you become a dedicated user it can take the place of nearly every other gadget in the kitchen. Or you can combine it with other tools to get the best out of them all.

When you first buy a food processor, take the time to get to know the machine. Find out what it can do. Put the attachments together and take them apart several times so that you can do that without thinking. Try out all the accessories to see for yourself what they can do. Then, in the early days, stop and think every time you start to prepare a dish: 'Which bits of this could I do in the food processor?', and *make* yourself use the machine instead of your old method.

As time goes on you will become more discriminating—if there are only a couple of courgettes to slice, or one small onion to chop, you will probably stick to your knife. But you can be sure you will never make onion soup again without your food processor—or a stew of mixed vegetables, or coleslaw. Use it for simple dishes as well as luxuries: it makes the smoothest possible sauce for a family supper of macaroni cheese, and the lightest pastry. If pâtés are something you have always bought for special occasions, because they are so tedious to make, think again. The food processor takes on all the chopping, mincing and mixing. In moments you are ready to bake the pâté and leave it to mature—certainly the professionals don't do all that mincing and mixing by hand.

Move on to baking and you will find you can whistle up a sandwich cake in no time, knead your bread dough in 10 seconds instead of 10 minutes, and mix and ice a glorious gâteau in the blink of an eyelid. If your food processor has a whisk attachment and variable speed control, you can also make a whisked sponge or meringues, and whip the cream to fill them.

Don't limit yourself to the recipes in this book to make use of your food processor. Adapt your own recipes, using the methods you will find here, and you will be happily surprised to see how quickly you have extended your repertoire of easy meals.

THE ATTACHMENTS

Different makes and models of food processor have different attachments, but the ranges are fairly similar. Check which are available for your particular model and make full use of them.

METAL BLADE
The basic attachment that comes with every food processor is a metal blade. This is the one that does all chopping, mincing and puréeing. It is *very* sharp and can tackle anything from grinding nuts to cutting the butter into the flour for pastry. Use it to chop onions or parsley, to mince meat and fish, to make breadcrumbs and purées. Take care when using this blade that you don't turn *everything* to a paste—it works with amazing speed.

PLASTIC BLADE
The plastic blade is the same shape as the metal one, but without the sharp edges. Use it for creaming cakes and for mixing doughs.

SLICING DISC
Some machines have different discs for thick and thin slices and alternative straight and crinkled edges. Other machines have only one slicing disc and rely on different pressures when you feed in the food to give you different thickness of slices. To slice foods, feed them in to the machine through the feeder tube while it is running, pressing them down with the pusher. Light pressure gives thinner slices; heavier pressure, thicker slices. Pack the feeder tube carefully to ensure even slices.

GRATING DISC
Discs with coarse and fine holes make for easy grating of vegetables and cheese. Again feed the food in through the feeder tube, pressing it gently with the pusher.

CHIPPER DISC
Take the chore out of making

potato chips with this disc, cutting the potatoes into neat, even chips in a flash. Try it with other large root vegetables too, such as turnips, sweet potatoes or swedes.

WHISK

A few machines have a whisk attachment for use with egg whites and cream. It is not quite as powerful as a conventional electric whisk but makes excellent soufflés, meringues and whipped cream. If you have a multi-speed or variable speed processor, you will achieve greater volume in egg whites and cream. You will also be able to continue using your processor for gently folding in all the ingredients, which is not possible in a single-speed machine. It really does eliminate the need for extra gadgets in the kitchen. Take care when washing the delicate plastic whisks.

JUICE EXTRACTOR

Some machines have a juice extractor, for citrus fruits and vegetables. It makes delicious drinks and flavourings.

PUSHER

The pusher is shaped to fit the feeder tube. Use it *always* to help you feed in foods for slicing and grating. *Never* use your fingers or a piece of equipment apart from the pusher; the machine works so fast you have no time to think how close you might be to the blade. Many manufacturers mark the pusher in millilitres or fluid ounces, so that you can also use it as a liquid measure, saving washing up.

SPATULA

A plastic spatula is provided which will not scratch the food processor bowl. You will find that you need to stop in the middle of some processes (such as creaming a cake mixture) to scrape down the bowl and bring the mixture back on to the blade; use the plastic spatula for this.

USING THE MACHINE

The food processor is extremely simple to use. Just choose the right attachment and the job is done almost before you know it. The one mistake most people make when they first start is over-processing. The machine works so fast they just can't believe that the meat is minced or the vegetable already puréed. Some machines are fitted with a variable speed switch, which will help you guard against this. Others work only at a constant speed. When working the latter type of machine, switch on and off quickly to give a pulse action. This usually supplies the best results when chopping and mixing, and enables you to check frequently the stage the food has reached—is it chopped finely enough for instance, or mixed smoothly enough? If you do not take the precaution of checking frequently, you will end up with everything turned to a fine paste—which is not always what you want.

Variable speed or multi-speed food processors are far easier to use than one with only a constant speed. It enables you to start processing slowly, working up to maximum speed as the job nears completion. This is particularly valuable when chopping with the metal blade or mixing solids into liquid for a sauce. With the machine working more slowly there is less danger of over-processing, and if a fine purée or smooth sauce are what you want there is less chance of finding occasional lumps of underprocessed food in the mixture.

Whatever type of machine you have, working it for too long is bad for the motor and will lead to overheating. This is particularly noticeable when mixing heavy doughs or large quantities of solid foods such as meat. Work in small batches to minimise the load on the motor and stop *as soon as the job is done.*

When using the metal blade, cut large pieces of food into chunks first: cut onions into quarters, meat into rough 2.5-cm (1-inch) chunks, bread into cubes. If you take butter straight from the refrigerator, cut it up with a knife as you put it in the bowl of the processor. Take care that you don't put in any bones with your meat. Don't try to process too much at a time, but work in batches—each batch only takes seconds anyway, so it is still quicker than working by conventional methods. Your manufacturer's booklet will give you a guide as to the machine's maximum weight capacity.

When puréeing soups, don't add too much liquid to the processor. Some machines have a liquid level mark on the bowl—don't fill it above that. If yours has no mark take care that the liquid does not come above the level of the central spindle. If you are making a large quantity of soup, you can either work in batches, or take the cooked solids out of the stock with a slotted spoon and purée them with a little liquid. Then you can mix the purée back into the stock in the saucepan. Variable or multi-speed food processors enable larger quantities of liquids to be processed at a time because the speed control prevents splashing.

Many people find it helpful to buy an extra bowl for the food processor, so that they do not have to stop and wash up a single bowl when switching from savoury to sweet ingredients or when making several dishes. But do remember there is no need to wash up the bowl between each operation if you do things in the right order. For instance, if you are making a savoury quiche, mix the pastry first, then chop the onion and vegetables, then mix the custard filling. The flavours blend in the finished dish anyway, so there is no need to wash the bowl after each item. You will of course have to wash it when you finish with savoury dishes and want to start a sweet dish. Even then a wipe with a damp cloth is often sufficient.

When you have finished with the machine, you will obviously want to wash both the bowl and attachments thoroughly. *Don't* drop the metal blade into a bowl of soapy water where you can't see it, or you are likely to cut your fingers; and *don't* put the whisk attachment in a dishwasher or washing up bowl—wash it separately. A brush is helpful for getting into the feeder tube and central spindle hole. Check the inside of the spindle if you have been mixing anything that may cling. Rinse under a running tap.

WHAT IT WON'T DO

There are a few things the food processor cannot tackle. It cannot, for instance, grind very hard spices to a powder, and it is not recommended for grinding coffee beans or crushing ice because these will blunt the metal blade and scratch the bowl. Neither is it successful with small quantities of tender herbs such as tarragon or chives; but parsley is the herb you probably use most and that is quite robust enough—chop it coarsely or finely, depending what you are using it for. And remember to include some of the stalk if it is for flavouring rather than just garnishing—the stalk is where most of the flavour lies.

SOME TIPS TO HELP YOU MAKE THE MOST OF YOUR MACHINE

When making pastry or scones in which the fat is cut into the flour, use hard butter or block margarine; cut it in pieces as you add it to the bowl. For creamed cake mixtures you can use either soft tub margarine or hard fat, but if it is hard, cut it up first.

When making cakes, best results are obtained by creaming the fat and sugar first, then adding the other ingredients stage by stage; that method gives you the lightest cake. Some books recommend putting all the ingredients in together and mixing all at once; this gives satisfactory results but not quite as good as if you mix in stages. If you have a variable or multi-speed processor

and a plastic blade, you can make cakes traditionally. On low speed you can gently *fold in* the flour and the fruit, completing the cake mix in the bowl. There is no need to sift flour; the food processor ensures that any lumps are thoroughly broken down, and other ingredients such as baking powder or cocoa are mixed in evenly.

STORING

Storing is something you shouldn't really do with your food processor—putting it away in a cupboard will tend to stop you getting the best out of it. Much better to leave it out on the working surface ready to swing into action at the touch of a switch. Some models come supplied with a plastic cover to stop it collecting dust. But you will of course need to store the attachments. Keep them as close as possible to the machine, either in the rack supplied by some makers or in a drawer or an open-topped box in the cupboard. Keep all the attachments together so that they are to hand when you need them. Store the pusher with the attachments rather than in place in the lid, so that air can circulate round the bowl and prevent smells developing.

STARTERS AND APPETISERS

POTTED STILTON WITH WALNUTS
BAGNA CAUDA
LIPTAUER CHEESE
AUBERGINE DIP
MUSHROOM CAVIARE
TARAMASALATA
HUMMUS
CHEESE STRAWS
SPINACH PÂTÉ
RILLETTES DE PORC
GUACAMOLE
SHRIMP PUFFS
TUNA-STUFFED TOMATOES
CHICKEN LIVER PÂTÉ

Potted Stilton with walnuts

METAL BLADE

100 g (4 oz) shelled walnuts
225 g (8 oz) Stilton cheese
75 g (3 oz) butter, softened
90 ml (6 tbsp) port

1

Fit the metal blade and chop the walnuts coarsely. Remove from the bowl and set aside.

2

Cut the cheese into chunks and put in the bowl with the butter and port. Mix to a smooth paste, using a pulse action.

3

Add the walnuts through the feeder tube and mix in very lightly using a pulse action. Take care not to over-process or the texture of the nuts will be lost.

4

Pack the cheese into an earthenware bowl, cover and chill. Serve with savoury crackers.

Makes about 450 g (1 lb)

Bagna cauda

METAL BLADE
PLASTIC BLADE

450 ml (15 fl oz) double cream
1 garlic clove, skinned
50-g (2-oz) can anchovy fillets,
  drained
5 ml (1 level tsp) dried thyme
5 ml (1 level tsp) dried oregano
pinch of sugar
40 g (1½ oz) butter

To serve
1 Cos lettuce, washed
1 bunch spring onions,
  trimmed
½ head celery, trimmed,
  washed and cut into sticks
3 red or green peppers, seeded
  and cut into strips
450 g (1 lb) broccoli, cut into
  florets
3 courgettes, cut into wedges
225 g (8 oz) mushrooms,
  quartered
225 g (8 oz) small tomatoes, cut
  into eighths
breadsticks

1

Arrange the prepared vegetables in a large shallow dish, cover and chill until ready to serve.

2

Put the cream in a saucepan and bring to the boil. Simmer, stirring, for 20 minutes, until reduced to about 300 ml (10 fl oz). Remove from the heat.

3

Meanwhile fit the metal blade and chop the garlic finely. Add the anchovies, thyme, oregano and sugar to the bowl and mix to a smooth paste.

4

Melt the butter in a small saucepan. Stir in the anchovy mixture and cook, stirring, for 10 minutes. Allow to cool a little.

5

Fit the plastic blade in the food processor and put the anchovy mixture in the bowl. Mixing at slow speed, or using a pulse action, add the warm cream through the feeder tube, mixing until smooth.

6

Pour the mixture into a fondue pot or flameproof dish and place over a spirit burner. Serve with the chilled vegetables and breadsticks.

Serves 12

Liptauer cheese

GRATING DISC
METAL BLADE

125 g (4 oz) Cheddar cheese
1 slice from a large onion
30 ml (2 tbsp) chopped fresh chives
225 g (8 oz) cottage cheese
125 g (4 oz) unsalted butter, softened
15 ml (1 tbsp) cider vinegar
5 ml (1 level tsp) French mustard
5 ml (1 level tsp) caraway seeds
5 ml (1 level tsp) paprika
1–2 anchovy fillets, drained
salt and freshly ground pepper (optional)

1

Fit the grating disc and grate the Cheddar cheese. Remove from the bowl and set aside.

2

Fit the metal blade and chop the onion finely. Return the Cheddar to the bowl and add the remaining ingredients, *except* the salt and pepper. Mix, starting at slow speed and increasing to maximum or using a pulse action. When the mixture is smooth, taste and add seasoning if necessary, mixing again briefly.

3

Divide the cheese between small dishes, cover and chill. Serve with savoury crackers.

Makes about 450 g (1 lb)

Aubergine dip

METAL BLADE

1 large aubergine
60 ml (4 tbsp) olive oil
1 medium onion, skinned and quartered
1 garlic clove, skinned
45 ml (3 tbsp) tahini paste
30 ml (2 tbsp) lemon juice
2.5 ml ($\frac{1}{2}$ level tsp) ground coriander
salt and freshly ground pepper
1 medium tomato, skinned, seeded and chopped
fresh coriander to garnish

1

Cut the aubergine in half lengthways. Score the flesh diagonally and dribble over 30 ml (2 tbsp) olive oil. Cook in the oven at 180°C (350°F) mark 4 for 1 hour or until flesh is soft.

2

Fit the metal blade and chop the onion and garlic. Cook in the remaining oil for about 5 minutes until softened.

3

Scoop out the aubergine flesh into the processor bowl and add the onion and garlic. Blend until smooth, increasing speed slowly or using a pulse action.

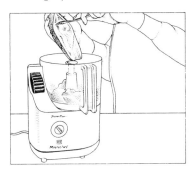

4

Add the tahini paste, lemon juice, coriander and season with salt and pepper. Stir in two-thirds of the chopped tomato and transfer to a serving bowl. Sprinkle over remaining tomato. Cover and chill. Garnish with fresh coriander and serve with fingers of hot buttered toast or pitta bread.

Serves 4

Mushroom caviare

METAL BLADE

1 large garlic clove, skinned
1 medium onion, skinned and
**   cut in chunks**
45 ml (3 tbsp) olive oil
450 g (1 lb) flat mushrooms,
**   trimmed and wiped**
pinch of ground mace
45 ml (3 tbsp) white wine
**   vinegar**
salt and freshly ground pepper
parsley to garnish

1

Fit the metal blade and chop the garlic finely. Add the onion and chop finely. Heat the oil in a saucepan, add the onion and garlic and fry gently for 8–10 minutes until soft but not starting to colour.

2

Meanwhile put the mushrooms in two batches in the food processor and chop roughly, using a pulse action. Add the chopped mushrooms to the pan, cover and cook gently, shaking the pan occasionally, for about 10 minutes until the mushrooms are soft. Allow to cool slightly.

3

Tip the mushroom mixture into the food processor. Add a pinch of mace, the vinegar and salt and pepper to taste. Chop finely, using a pulse action, without reducing the mixture to a purée. Check the seasoning, spoon into a serving bowl and chill.

4

With the metal blade, chop the parsley finely; garnish the mushroom 'caviare' with parsley just before serving. Serve with savoury crackers or toast fingers.

Makes 450 g (1 lb)

Mushroom caviare

Mushrooms have been cultivated with varying degrees of success since 1650, but it's only comparatively recently that we've come fully to understand and control the production of this mysterious semi-vegetable. What the cook has to remember, though, is simple enough: the bigger and flatter the cap, the more fully developed the mushroom will be, and hence the more 'mushroomy' will be the flavour. Button mushrooms are best used when presentation is at a premium: their flavour is much milder.

Taramasalata

METAL BLADE

75 g (3 oz) bread
1 garlic clove, skinned
1 small onion, skinned and
**   quartered**
225 g (8 oz) cod's roe, skinned
grated rind and juice of 1
**   lemon**
150 ml ($\frac{1}{4}$ pint) olive oil
freshly ground pepper
olives and parsley to garnish

1

Remove the crusts from the bread.

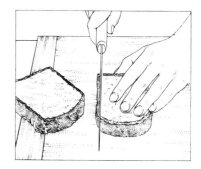

2

Cut the bread into chunks. Fit the metal blade and chop the bread to fine crumbs; remove and set aside.

3

Chop the garlic finely, then add the onion and chop. Finally add the cod's roe, breadcrumbs, lemon rind and juice; mix to a purée, starting at slow speed and increasing to maximum, or using a pulse action.

4

Gradually add the oil through the feeder tube, mixing well after each addition. Then add 90 ml (6 tbsp) hot water and season with pepper. Garnish with olives and a small sprig of parsley.

Serves 6–8

Hummus

METAL BLADE

225 g (8 oz) chick peas
salt and freshly ground pepper
1–2 garlic cloves, skinned
90 ml (6 tbsp) lemon juice
45 ml (3 level tbsp) sesame
**   seeds**
30 ml (2 level tbsp) cumin
**   seeds**
300 ml ($\frac{1}{2}$ pint) olive oil
paprika to garnish
pitta bread to serve

1

Wash the peas, cover with cold water and leave to soak for 12 hours or overnight.

2

Drain the water off, place the peas in a saucepan and cover with cold water. Bring to the boil and simmer gently for 2 hours or until tender. Add more boiling water if necessary to keep the peas covered with water throughout the cooking time; add 5 ml (1 level tsp) salt 10 minutes before cooking is finished. Drain and reserve a few whole peas for garnish.

3

Fit the metal blade and chop the garlic finely. Add all but the reserved peas, the lemon juice, sesame seeds and cumin seeds. Chop to a fine purée. Gradually add the oil, reserving 15 ml (1 tbsp) through the feeder tube, blending well after each addition. Season with salt and pepper to taste and mix briefly again. Spoon into a serving bowl and sprinkle with the reserved oil. Garnish with the reserved whole chick peas and sprinkle with paprika. Serve with warm pitta bread.

Serves 8

Hummus

Hummus, or to give it its full Arab name *Hummus-bi-tahini*, is a traditional Middle Eastern dip, generally served as part of a *mezzeh*. *Mezzeh* has been described as 'a large collection of little things': very much part of Arab life, it finds its counterpart in the Scandinavian *smörgåsbord*, the French *hors d'oeuvre*, the Spanish *tapas*, and the Greek *mezes*. In happier days, Lebanon was the gastronomic capital of the *mezzeh*, and restaurants in Lebanese mountain resorts would routinely provide a *mezzeh* of 200 or so items for their customers. Hummus would always be prominent: it is as delicious and perennially popular as it is nutritious.

Cheese straws

GRATING DISC
METAL BLADE

**50 g (2 oz) mature Cheddar
cheese
100 g (4 oz) plain flour
salt and cayenne pepper
50 g (2 oz) butter or block
margarine
1 egg yolk
cold water to mix**

1

Fit the coarse grating disc and
grate the cheese; remove and set
the cheese aside.

2

Change to the metal blade. Put
the flour, salt and a pinch of
cayenne in the bowl and mix
briefly. Add the fat, cut in small
pieces, and mix on high speed
until the mixture resembles fine
breadcrumbs. Add the grated
cheese and mix again briefly.

3

With the machine on slow speed,
or using a pulse action, add the
egg yolk through the feeder tube,
then add enough cold water to
form a stiff dough. Mix just until a
smooth dough forms.

4

Roll out the pastry thinly and trim
to oblongs 18 cm (7 inches) long
and 6.5 cm (2½ inches) wide. Place
on a greased baking sheet and cut
each into straws 6.5 cm (2½ inches)
long and 0.5 cm (¼ inch) wide,
separating them as you cut.

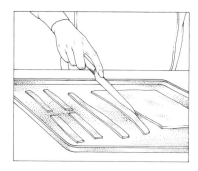

5

Bake in the oven at 200°C (400°F)
mark 6 for 10–15 minutes until
pale golden in colour. Remove
from the oven and cool slightly on
a wire rack.

Makes about 80 straws

Spinach pâté

SLICING DISC
GRATING DISC
METAL BLADE

**1 bunch spring onions,
trimmed
2 large carrots, peeled
700 g (1½ lb) frozen chopped
spinach, thawed
50 g (2 oz) butter or block
margarine
100 ml (4 fl oz) single cream
100 ml (4 fl oz) milk
8.75 ml (1¾ level tsp) salt
5 ml (1 level tsp) dried basil
pinch cayenne pepper
4 eggs, beaten
watercress sprigs to garnish**

1

Fit the slicing disc and slice the
spring onions thinly. Change to
the coarse grating disc and grate
the carrots. Remove from the bowl
and set aside.

2

Put the spinach in a colander in
the sink and press it firmly with
the back of a wooden spoon to
drain out the liquid. Then squeeze
it by hand to remove any
remaining moisture. Fit the metal
blade and chop the drained
spinach very finely.

3

Melt the fat, add the spring onions
and carrots and cook, stirring
frequently, for about 5 minutes,
until the onions are soft but not
coloured. Stir in the spinach,
cream, milk, salt, basil and
cayenne. Bring to the boil, then

remove the saucepan from the heat and stir in the eggs.

4

Grease a 450-g (1-lb) loaf tin and line the base with foil.

5

Spoon the mixture into the prepared loaf tin, spreading it evenly, and cover with foil. Stand the tin in a roasting tin and add hot water to come 2.5 cm (1 inch) up the sides of the loaf tin. Bake in the oven at 190°C (375°F) mark 5 for 1¼ hours or until a knife inserted through the foil into the pâté comes out clean.

6

Place the loaf tin on a wire rack to cool for 15 minutes, then place two heavy cans on top of the foil to weight it down. Chill overnight.

7

To serve, remove the weights and foil from the top of the pâté and loosen it from the sides of the tin with a palette knife dipped in hot water. Turn the pâté out on to a flat plate and remove the foil. Garnish with watercress sprigs and cut the pâté into thick slices.

Serves 10

Rillettes de porc

METAL BLADE

900 g (2 lb) belly or shoulder of pork
salt
450 g (1 lb) pork fat
1 garlic clove, skinned and bruised
bouquet garni
75 ml (5 tbsp) water
freshly ground pepper
fresh bay leaves to garnish
toasted French bread to serve

1

Remove the rind and bones from the pork belly or shoulder.

2

Rub the meat well with salt and leave it to stand for about 4–6 hours.

3

Cut the meat into strips along the grooves from where the bones were removed and cut the fat into strips. Put the meat and fat into an ovenproof dish with the garlic, bouquet garni and water and season with plenty of pepper.

Cover and cook in the oven at 150°C (300°F) mark 2 for about 4 hours.

4

Remove from the oven, discard the bouquet garni and garlic and season the meat well. Strain off and discard the fat. Fit the metal blade and chop very roughly in batches, using a pulse action.

5

Spoon the meat into an earthenware dish, packing it down well. Cover and chill until required. Garnish with fresh bay leaves and serve with toasted French bread.

Serves 6

Guacamole

METAL BLADE

2 avocados
1 garlic clove, skinned
½ small onion, skinned
1 tomato, skinned and seeded
30 ml (2 tbsp) lemon juice
6.25 ml (1¼ level tsp) salt
2.5–5 ml (½–1 level tsp) chilli powder
fresh coriander leaves (optional) to garnish
potato crisps to serve

1

Cut the avocados in half lengthways, remove the stones and peel.

2

Fit the metal blade and chop the garlic finely. Add the onion and chop finely. Add the avocados and remaining ingredients and chop to a smooth purée.

3

Spoon the mixture into a bowl and garnish with coriander leaves if you wish. Serve with potato crisps.

Makes 450 ml (¾ pint)

Shrimp puffs

METAL BLADE

15 g (½ oz) butter or block margarine
15 ml (1 level tbsp) flour
50 ml (2 fl oz) milk
1 egg, beaten
sprig of parsley
1 small gherkin
75 g (3 oz) peeled shrimps
15 ml (1 tbsp) lemon juice
5 ml (1 level tsp) grated lemon rind
salt and freshly ground pepper
dash of Tabasco sauce
212 g (7½ oz) frozen puff pastry, thawed
milk to glaze
lemon wedges and parsley to garnish

1

Fit the metal blade and place the butter and flour in the bowl. Mix until blended then pour in the milk and mix using a pulse action until smooth. Pour into a saucepan and gradually bring to the boil, stirring continuously until the sauce thickens. Simmer for a further 2–3 minutes. Remove from the heat.

2

Put the parsley and gherkin in the processor and chop finely. Stir into the sauce with the beaten egg, shrimps, lemon juice and rind, seasoning and Tabasco sauce.

3

Roll out the pastry and divide into six 7.5-cm (3-inch) squares.

Use a ruler to measure out the pastry squares evenly and cut with a sharp knife.

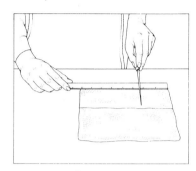

4

Divide the filling equally between the pastry squares, dampen the edges with water and fold in half to form a triangle. Seal the edges and place on a greased baking tray. Glaze with the milk.

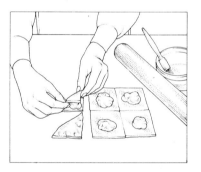

5

Bake in the oven at 200°C (400°F) mark 6 for 30 minutes until well risen and golden brown. Serve hot, garnished with lemon wedges and sprigs of parsley.

Serves 6

TUNA STUFFED TOMATOES
PAGE 19

SMOKED SALMON MOUSSE
PAGE 22

Tuna-stuffed tomatoes

METAL BLADE
SLICING DISC

6 large, ripe tomatoes
salt and freshly ground pepper
fresh parsley
12 black olives, stoned
200-g ($7\frac{1}{2}$-oz) can tuna, drained
2 eggs, hard-boiled, shelled and halved
90 ml (6 tbsp) mayonnaise
1 cucumber
paprika to garnish

1

Slice the rounded end off each tomato and reserve. Scoop out the middles with a teaspoon. Season inside with salt and pepper.

2

Fit the metal blade and chop the parsley; remove and set aside. Chop the olives. Add the tuna to the bowl with the eggs, mayonnaise and 30 ml (2 tbsp) chopped parsley. Mix, using a pulse action and taking care not to over-process.

3

Spoon some of the mixture into each tomato, heaping it up well, and place each one on an individual plate.

4

Fit the slicing disc and slice the cucumber. Arrange a circle of cucumber slices round each tomato and dust with paprika.

Serves 6

Chicken liver pâté

METAL BLADE

700 g ($1\frac{1}{2}$ lb) chicken livers
75 g (3 oz) butter or block margarine
1 large garlic clove, skinned
1 onion, skinned and quartered
15 ml (1 tbsp) double cream
30 ml (2 level tbsp) tomato purée
45 ml (3 tbsp) sherry or brandy
sprig of parsley to garnish

1

Rinse the chicken livers in cold water and dry them thoroughly with absorbent kitchen paper. Melt the butter in a frying pan and fry the livers, stirring occasionally, for about 10 minutes until they change colour.

2

Fit the metal blade and chop the garlic finely. Add the onion and chop finely. Reduce the heat under the frying pan and add the garlic and onion. Cover and cook for about 5 minutes, then remove them from the heat and leave to cool slightly. Stir in the double cream, tomato purée and the sherry or brandy.

3

Turn the mixture into the food processor half at a time and chop to a smooth purée. Turn it into a small bowl and chill until required. Garnish with parsley.

Serves 10

LIGHT DISHES

Coarse Garlic Pâté

Spanish Omelette

Smoked Salmon Mousse

Quiche Lorraine

Spinach Soufflé

Courgette Quiche

Golden Haddock Soufflé

Cheese and Spinach Pie

Cheese and Bacon Soufflé

Pizza Napoletana

Individual Asparagus Soufflés

Spinach Pancakes

Coarse garlic pâté

METAL BLADE

225 g (8 oz) pigs liver
30 ml (2 tbsp) milk
50 g (2 oz) mushrooms, wiped
2 garlic cloves, skinned
1 small onion, skinned and quartered
225 g (8 oz) belly pork
125 g (4 oz) pork fat
125 g (4 oz) stewing steak
30 ml (2 tbsp) red wine
pinch of grated nutmeg
salt and freshly ground pepper

1

Make the pâté 2 days before it is needed. Soak the liver in the milk for about 1 hour, then drain.

2

Fit the metal blade and roughly chop the mushrooms; remove and set aside.

3

Chop the garlic finely, then add the onion and chop finely. Cut the drained liver, the belly pork, pork fat and stewing steak into 2.5-cm (1-inch) chunks and add to the bowl with the wine, nutmeg, salt and pepper. Chop, using short bursts, until the meats are coarsely minced; do not over-process or the mixture will turn to a paste.

4

Add the chopped mushrooms and mix in briefly (you should still be able to see pieces of mushroom in the mixture).

5

Pack the mixture tightly into a 1-litre (1¾-pint) terrine, cover with foil or a lid and place in a roasting tin half filled with boiling water. Cook in the oven at 170°C (325°F) mark 3 for about 2 hours.

6

When cooked cover the pâté with foil and weight down. When cold, refrigerate until required. Turn the pâté out of the tin and let it come to at room temperature for 30 minutes before serving.

Serves 8

Spanish omelette

METAL BLADE

2 large onions, skinned and cut in chunks
1 red pepper, quartered and seeds removed
45 ml (3 tbsp) olive oil
2 large potatoes, peeled and cut in 1-cm (½-inch) cubes
salt and freshly ground pepper
6 eggs, lightly beaten

1

Fit the metal blade and coarsely chop the onions and red pepper. In a medium sized frying pan, gently heat the olive oil. Add the potatoes, onions and red pepper and season with salt and pepper. Sauté, stirring occasionally, for 10–15 minutes until golden brown.

2

Drain off excess oil and quickly stir in the eggs. Cook for 5 minutes, shaking the pan occasionally to prevent sticking. If you wish, place under a hot grill to brown the top. Turn the omelette out on to a warmed serving plate.

Serves 4

Smoked salmon mousse

METAL BLADE
WHISK

300 ml ($\frac{1}{2}$ pint) milk
1 small carrot, peeled and
    halved
1 small onion, skinned and
    halved
3 parsley stalks
6 peppercorns
40 g (1$\frac{1}{2}$ oz) butter
25 g (1 oz) flour
175 g (6 oz) smoked salmon
    trimmings
25 ml (5 level tsp) gelatine
450 ml ($\frac{3}{4}$ pint) chicken stock
300 ml (10 fl oz) double cream
juice of $\frac{1}{2}$ lemon
30 ml (2 level tbsp)
    mayonnaise
salt and freshly ground pepper
lemon slices and extra smoked
    salmon to garnish
Melba toast to serve

1

Pour the milk into a saucepan, add the carrot, onion, parsley stalks and peppercorns. Bring to the boil, remove from the heat and allow to infuse for 15 minutes. Melt the butter in another saucepan.

2

Fit the metal blade and put the butter and flour in the bowl; strain in the milk and discard the flavourings. Mix, starting on slow speed and increasing to maximum, or using a pulse action,

until smooth. Pour into a saucepan and bring to the boil, stirring. Simmer for 5 minutes, stirring occasionally; remove from the heat. Cover the surface of the sauce with cling film and cool it.

3

Put 45 ml (3 tbsp) stock in a bowl and sprinkle the gelatine over; leave for a few minutes to soften. Then place the bowl in a pan of hot water until the gelatine is dissolved. Stir in the rest of the chicken stock.

4

Fit the whisk and whip the cream lightly. Transfer it to another bowl and set aside. Change to the metal blade and put the cold sauce, gelatine mixture, smoked salmon, lemon juice and mayonnaise in the bowl. Mix until smooth and well blended. Add the whipped cream and mix again briefly.

5

Pour the mixture into a 1.1-litre (2-pint) soufflé dish or fish mould. Chill until set. Dip the container in hot water and invert on to a serving plate. Garnish with lemon wedges and curly endive. Serve with Melba toast.

Serves 8

Quiche lorraine

METAL BLADE
SLICING DISC

75–100 g (3–4 oz) lean bacon,
    rinded
2 eggs
150 ml (5 fl oz) single cream or
    milk
75–100 g (3–4 oz) Gruyère
    cheese
salt and freshly ground pepper
shortcrust pastry made with
    150 g (5 oz) plain flour (see
    page 119)

1

Fit the metal blade and chop the bacon roughly. Transfer it to a bowl, cover with boiling water and leave for 2–3 minutes then drain well. Put the eggs and cream or milk in the food processor and mix well; pour into another bowl, season and set aside. Change to the slicing disc and slice the cheese thinly.

2

Roll out the pastry and use it to line an 18-cm (7-inch) plain flan ring, placed on a baking sheet. Chill in the refrigerator for 30 minutes.

3

Prick the base of the pastry case with a fork, then line with foil or greaseproof paper and baking beans and bake blind in the oven at 200°C (400°F) mark 6 for 10–15 minutes until set. Remove the foil and beans.

4

Put the drained bacon into the pastry case with the cheese and pour in the eggs and cream.

5

Bake in the oven at 180°C (350°F) mark 4 for a further 30 minutes, until well risen and golden.

Serves 4

Spinach soufflé

GRATING DISC
METAL BLADE
WHISK

450 g (1 lb) trimmed fresh spinach or 226-g (8-oz) packet frozen chopped spinach
25 g (1 oz) Parmesan cheese
40 g (1½ oz) onion, skinned and quartered
40 g (1½ oz) butter or block margarine
25 g (1 oz) flour
10–12.5 ml (2–2½ level tsp) salt
1.25 ml (¼ level tsp) cayenne pepper
350 ml (12 fl oz) milk
6 eggs, separated

1

Grease a 1.8-litre (3¼-pint) soufflé dish. Prepare and cook the spinach. If using fresh spinach, wash it well in several waters to remove all the grit. Pack into a saucepan with only the water that clings to the leaves. Heat gently, turning the spinach occasionally, then bring to the boil and cook for 5–10 minutes or until tender. For frozen spinach, cook according to the instructions on the packet and drain thoroughly.

2

Meanwhile, fit the fine grating disc and grate the Parmesan cheese; remove from the bowl and set aside. Fit the metal blade and chop the onion; remove from the bowl and set aside. If using fresh spinach, when it is cooked drain thoroughly and chop finely in the food processor fitted with the metal blade.

3

Melt the butter or margarine in a large saucepan, add the onion and fry for 5 minutes. Stir in the flour, salt and cayenne and cook gently, stirring, until smooth. Slowly add the milk and cook, stirring, until the sauce is thickened.

4

Mix the egg yolks together lightly and beat in a little of the hot sauce; slowly pour the egg mixture into the sauce, stirring rapidly. Cook over low heat, stirring, until thickened; do not boil. Remove from the heat and stir in the spinach and cheese.

5

Fit the whisk and whisk the egg whites until stiff then gently fold into the spinach mixture with a large metal spoon. Pour into the soufflé dish and bake in the oven at 190°C (375°F) mark 5 for 40–45 minutes until well risen and golden brown. Serve immediately.

Serves 6

Courgette quiche

GRATING DISC
METAL BLADE
SLICING DISC

350 g (12 oz) courgettes, wiped and trimmed
salt
6 leaves of fresh basil or 5 ml (1 level tsp) dried basil
3 eggs
150 ml (5 fl oz) double cream
finely grated rind of 1 lime (optional)
freshly ground pepper

Cheese pastry
125 g (4 oz) Cheddar cheese
175 g (6 oz) plain flour
salt
125 g (4 oz) butter or block margarine
1 egg yolk, beaten

1

Make the cheese pastry. Fit the grating disc and grate the cheese; remove and set aside. Fit the metal blade and put the flour and a pinch of salt in the bowl; mix briefly. Cut the butter in small pieces, add to the bowl and mix on high speed, using a pulse action, until the mixture resembles fine breadcrumbs. Add the grated cheese and mix again briefly. With the machine on slow speed, or using a pulse action, add the egg yolk and mix just until a smooth dough forms. Roll out the pastry on a floured surface and use to line a loose-bottomed 23-cm (9-inch) flan tin. Chill in the refrigerator for 30 minutes.

2

Fit the slicing disc and slice the courgettes then set aside. Fit the metal blade and if using fresh basil, chop finely. Add the eggs, cream, dried basil, the lime rind if using, and salt and pepper to taste. Mix briefly.

3

Prick the base of the pastry case with a fork, then line with foil or greaseproof paper and baking beans and bake blind in the oven at 200°C (400°F) mark 6 for 10–15 minutes until set. Remove the foil and beans.

4

Place the courgette slices in the pastry case, then pour in the egg and cream mixture. Return it to the oven for a further 20 minutes or until the filling is set. Leave to stand for 15 minutes before serving warm.

Serves 6

Golden haddock soufflé

METAL BLADE
GRATING DISC
WHISK

225 ml (8 fl oz) milk
25 g (1 oz) butter or block margarine
25 g (1 oz) flour
75 g (3 oz) Red Leicester cheese
small bunch of fresh chives, chopped
salt and freshly ground pepper
3 eggs, separated
100 g (4 oz) smoked haddock, cooked and flaked

1

Lightly grease a 1.4-litre (2½-pint) soufflé dish. Pour the milk into a saucepan and bring to the boil. Remove from the heat.

2

Fit the metal blade and place the butter and flour in the bowl. Mix until blended then pour in the milk and mix, using a pulse action, until smooth. Pour into the saucepan and bring to the boil, stirring. Simmer for 2–3 minutes, stirring occasionally until the sauce has thickened. Cool slightly.

3

Fit the grating disc and grate the cheese; remove and set aside. Add the cheese and 30 ml (2 tbsp) chives to the sauce with the seasoning, egg yolks and fish.

4

Fit the whisk and stiffly whisk the egg whites. Fold them into the fish mixture with a large metal spoon, then pour into the soufflé dish. Bake in the oven at 200°C (400°F) mark 6 for 35 minutes until well risen and golden brown. Serve the soufflé immediately.

Serves 4

Cheese and spinach pie

GRATING DISC
METAL BLADE

225 g (8 oz) Mozzarella or Bel Paese cheese
100 g (4 oz) curd cheese
226-g (8-oz) packet frozen chopped spinach, thawed and drained well
pinch of garlic salt
freshly ground pepper
3 eggs
shortcrust pastry made with 200 g (7 oz) plain flour (see page 119)

1

Fit the grating disc and grate the cheese. Change to the metal blade and add the curd cheese, spinach, garlic salt and pepper. Separate 1 egg and reserve the yolk; add the white and the remaining eggs to the bowl. Mix, starting at slow speed and increasing to maximum, or using a pulse action.

2

Divide the pastry into two pieces, one slightly larger than the other. Roll out the larger piece and use to line an 18-cm (7-inch) flan dish or tin, or deep pie plate. Spoon the filling on to the pastry.

3

Roll out the remaining pastry for the lid until it is 1 cm ($\frac{1}{2}$ inch) larger than the rim of the dish. Brush the pastry rim with water then lift the lid into position. Trim and seal, knock up and scallop the edge.

Use the pastry trimmings to make leaf shapes, decorate the pie with them and glaze with the reserved egg yolk beaten with a little water.

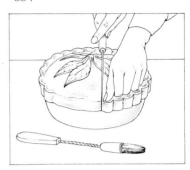

4

Bake in the oven at 190°C (375°F) mark 5 for 1$\frac{1}{4}$ hours, or until the pastry is golden and well glazed. Leave the pie to stand for at least 10 minutes to set slightly before slicing it. Serve hot or cold.

Serves 4

Cheese and bacon soufflé

GRATING DISC
METAL BLADE
WHISK

100 g (4 oz) Cheddar cheese
2 rashers streaky bacon, rinded
225 ml (8 fl oz) evaporated milk or milk
40 g (1½ oz) butter or block margarine
30 ml (2 level tbsp) flour
salt and freshly ground pepper
3 eggs, separated

1

Butter a 1.4-litre (2½-pint) soufflé dish. Fit the grating disc and grate the cheese; remove and set aside. Fit the metal blade and chop the bacon. Fry the bacon in its own fat until crisp. Set aside.

2

Pour the milk into a saucepan and bring to the boil.

3

Fit the metal blade and place the butter and flour in the bowl. Mix until well blended then pour in the hot milk and mix, using a pulse action, until smooth.

4

Pour into the saucepan and bring to the boil, stirring. Simmer for 2–3 minutes, stirring occasionally, until the sauce has thickened. Remove from the heat and stir in the grated cheese and seasoning. Cool a little, then mix the egg yolks together and beat into the sauce, a little at a time. Stir until well blended. Set aside.

5

Fit the whisk and whisk the egg whites until stiff. Fold them into the cheese mixture with the bacon pieces, using a large metal spoon.

6

Pour into the soufflé dish and bake in the oven at 180°C (350°F) mark 4 for 40–50 minutes, or until well risen and golden.

Serves 4

Pizza napoletana

PLASTIC BLADE
METAL BLADE

7.5 ml (1½ level tsp) dried yeast and a pinch of sugar *or* 15 g (½ oz) fresh yeast
150 ml (¼ pint) warm water
225 g (8 oz) strong plain flour
5 ml (1 level tsp) salt
small knob of lard
vegetable oil

For topping
225 g (8 oz) onions, skinned and quartered
olive oil
two 425-g (15-oz) cans tomatoes, drained
10 ml (2 level tsp) dried marjoram
salt and freshly ground pepper
175 g (6 oz) Bel Paese
two 50-g (2-oz) cans anchovy fillets, drained
black olives

1

Sprinkle the dried yeast into the water with the sugar. Leave in a warm place for 15 minutes until frothy. For fresh yeast, blend with water and use at once; omit sugar.

2

Fit the plastic blade. Put the flour, salt and lard in the bowl and mix on maximum speed for a few seconds. Switch to slow speed, or use a pulse action, and add the yeast liquid through the feeder tube. Gradually increase the speed to maximum and mix until a dough forms. Cover the bowl with a clean teatowel and leave in a warm place until doubled in size.

3

Turn the dough on to a floured surface and roll into a long strip. Brush with oil and roll it up like a Swiss roll. Repeat 3 times.

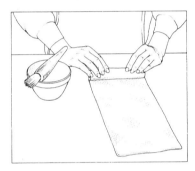

4

Roll out the dough to a 30-cm (12-inch) round, place on a greased baking sheet and pinch up a rim round the edge. Brush with oil.

5

Fit the metal blade and chop the onions finely. Sauté them in a little oil until soft. Spread to within 2 cm ($\frac{3}{4}$ inch) of the edge of the dough. Arrange the tomatoes on top, sprinkle with seasoning and bake in the oven at 230°C (450°F) mark 8 for 20 minutes.

6

With the metal blade, chop the Bel Paese cheese roughly. Scatter the cheese over the pizza, lattice it with anchovies and arrange olives in the spaces between. Cover with foil and cook for 20 minutes.

Serves 6

Individual asparagus soufflés

GRATING DISC
METAL BLADE
WHISK

225 g (8 oz) asparagus
100 g (4 oz) Cheddar cheese
50 g (2 oz) butter or block margarine
60 ml (4 level tbsp) flour
5 ml (1 level tsp) salt
350 ml (12 fl oz) milk
6 eggs, separated
2.5 ml ($\frac{1}{2}$ level tsp) white pepper
5 ml (1 level tsp) dry mustard

1

Cook the asparagus in a deep-frying basket or colander, in boiling salted water, until just tender.

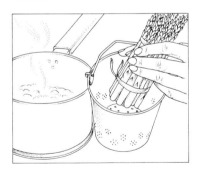

2

Drain the asparagus well and cut into small chunks. Fit the grating disc and grate the cheese; remove and set aside.

3

Fit the metal blade. Melt the butter then put it in the food processor with the flour, salt and milk; blend thoroughly, starting on slow speed and increasing to maximum.

4

Pour into a large saucepan and cook, stirring, until thickened. Add the asparagus and remove from the heat. Mix the egg yolks together and beat in a little of the hot sauce. Slowly pour the egg mixture into the sauce, stirring rapidly. Stir in the pepper, mustard and cheese and set aside.

5

Fit the whisk and whisk the egg whites until stiff. Fold them into the asparagus mixture with a large metal spoon. Spoon into eight greased 150-ml ($\frac{1}{4}$-pint) ramekins and bake in the oven at 170°C (325°F) mark 3 for about 30 minutes or until well risen and lightly golden.

Serves 8

Spinach pancakes

METAL BLADE
GRATING DISC

125 g (4 oz) plain flour
pinch of salt
1 egg
300 ml ($\frac{1}{2}$ pint) milk
lard for frying

Filling
350 g (12 oz) frozen chopped
   spinach or 700 g (1$\frac{1}{2}$ lb) fresh
   spinach, trimmed
75 g (3 oz) Gruyère cheese
25 g (1 oz) butter or block
   margarine
20 ml (4 level tsp) flour
salt and freshly ground pepper
150 ml ($\frac{1}{4}$ pint) milk
45 ml (3 tbsp) single cream

1

Fit the metal blade. Put the flour and salt in the bowl and mix briefly. Add the egg and half the milk and mix until smooth, starting on slow speed and increasing to maximum, or using a pulse action. Add the remaining milk through the feeder tube and mix again until thoroughly blended.

2

Heat a little lard in an 18-cm (7-inch) heavy frying pan and swirl it round to coat the sides of the pan; pour off and reserve the surplus. Raise the handle side of the pan slightly and pour in a little batter from the raised side so that it flows over the pan. Place over a moderate heat and cook until

golden underneath. Turn with a palette knife and cook the other side. Slide the pancake on to a plate and keep hot. Repeat with the remaining batter to make 8 thin pancakes.

3

Cook the frozen spinach according to the instructions on the packet and drain well; or cook the fresh spinach (see page 23), drain and chop finely in the food processor. Remove and set aside.

4

Melt the butter in a large saucepan and put it in the food processor with the flour, salt, pepper, milk and cream. Mix thoroughly, starting on slow speed and increasing to maximum. Pour into the saucepan. Cook gently until the sauce is thickened, stirring constantly.

5

Fit the grating disc and grate the cheese. Add the cooked spinach and grated cheese to the sauce. Warm through, stirring, until the cheese is melted.

6

Spoon about 60 ml (4 tbsp) of the filling into the centre of each

pancake. Fold one edge over the filling and roll up carefully. Arrange the finished pancakes on a serving dish and serve hot.

Serves 4

SOUPS

Broccoli and Orange Soup

Bortsch

Greek Egg and Lemon Soup

Cream of Spinach Soup

Curried Carrot Soup

French Onion Soup

Mediterranean Fish Soup with Aïoli

Iced Cucumber and Mint Soup

Lettuce Soup

Vichyssoise (chilled leek and potato)

Walnut and Mushroom Soup

Shropshire Pea and Ham Soup

Iced Tomato Soup with Fresh Basil

Goulash Soup

Crab Bisque

Gazpacho

Seafood Gumbo

Broccoli orange soup

SLICING DISC
METAL BLADE

1 medium onion, skinned
25 g (1 oz) butter or block
margarine
600 ml (1 pint) chicken stock
900 g (2 lb) broccoli, trimmed
juice of 1 orange
salt and freshly ground pepper
60 ml (4 tbsp) double cream
2 thin orange slices, halved, to
garnish

1

Fit the slicing disc and slice the onion. Melt the butter in a large saucepan, add the onion and fry gently for 5 minutes until soft.

2

Add the stock, broccoli, orange juice and seasoning. Cover and simmer for 20 minutes until the broccoli is tender.

3

Allow the soup to cool a little, then fit the metal blade and purée the soup half at a time, using a pulse action.

4

Return it to the pan and heat through. Remove from the heat and stir in the cream. Garnish each bowl with a slice of orange.

Serves 4

Borscht

GRATING DISC
METAL BLADE

6 small raw beetroot (about
1 kg, 2¼ lb)
2 medium onions, skinned and
quartered
1.1 litres (2 pints) beef stock
30 ml (2 tbsp) lemon juice
90 ml (6 tbsp) dry sherry
salt and freshly ground pepper
142 ml (5 fl oz) soured cream
30 ml (2 tbsp) chopped fresh
chives to garnish

1

Peel the six beetroot.

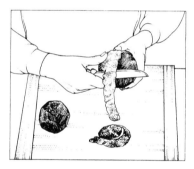

2

Fit the grating disc and grate the beetroot coarsely. Remove from the bowl and put it in a large saucepan.

3

Fit the metal blade and chop the onion. Add to the saucepan, with the stock. Bring to the boil and simmer without a lid for about 45 minutes.

4

Strain and add the lemon juice and sherry. Adjust the seasoning.

Serve either well chilled or hot, with a whirl of soured cream and chopped chives on each portion.

Serves 4

Borscht

Beetroot is a flavourful and beautiful vegetable sadly neglected in this country: its vivid colour and delicately sweet flavour have a huge variety of uses in the kitchen. One of the finest of these is for Borscht, a Polish soup widely made all across Eastern and Central Europe. Borscht is the pride of Old Polish cooking, and the oldest surviving recipe dates from the beginning of the sixteenth century.

There are two classical versions of Borscht: one made with a vegetable stock which is served on Christmas Eve, and the other made with a meat stock, served at Easter. This recipe is closest to the second.

Greek egg and lemon soup

METAL BLADE
PLASTIC BLADE

2 shallots, skinned and halved
25 g (1 oz) butter or margarine
1.1 litres (2 pints) chicken stock
pared rind and juice of $\frac{1}{2}$
**   lemon**
50 g (2 oz) long grain rice
2 eggs
salt and freshly ground pepper

1

Fit the metal blade and chop the shallots. Melt the butter in a saucepan, add the shallots and fry gently for 7–8 minutes until soft but not coloured.

2

Add the chicken stock and lemon rind and bring to the boil. Add the rice and boil gently, uncovered, for 10—12 minutes until the rice is just tender.

3

Fit the plastic blade to the food processor and very briefly beat together the eggs and lemon juice, until just mixed. Add a ladleful of the hot stock through the feeder tube and mix again.

4

Pour the egg mixture into the saucepan and heat through gently, stirring continuously. Do not allow to boil or the egg will

curdle. Season to taste and serve the soup immediately.

Serves 4–6

Cream of spinach soup

METAL BLADE

1 medium onion, skinned and
**   quartered**
50 g (2 oz) butter
175-g (6-oz) packet frozen
**   spinach (leaves or chopped),**
**   thawed and well drained**
25 g (1 oz) flour
300 ml ($\frac{1}{2}$ pint) chicken stock
about 568 ml (1 pint) milk
salt and freshly ground pepper
pinch of grated nutmeg
30 ml (2 tbsp) single cream

1

Fit the metal blade and chop the onion finely. Melt the butter in a large saucepan and gently fry the onion and spinach for 5–6 minutes. Add the flour and stir thoroughly; remove from the heat.

2

Gradually stir in the stock and milk. Return to the heat and bring to the boil, stirring continuously, until the mixture thickens. Cover and simmer for 15–20 minutes; season to taste.

3

Allow the soup to cool a little then purée it half at a time using a pulse action. Return it to the saucepan and if necessary, thin it with a little more milk. Reheat gently. Pour into a warmed soup tureen or individual dishes and stir in the cream just before serving.

Serves 4

Curried carrot soup

METAL BLADE

**350 g (12 oz) carrots, peeled
  and cut in chunks**
**1 Spanish onion, skinned and
  cut in chunks**
1 garlic clove, skinned
30 ml (2 tbsp) vegetable oil
**5 ml (1 level tsp) ground
  coriander**
5 ml (1 level tsp) ground cumin
**5 ml (1 level tsp) ground
  turmeric**
**1.25 ml ($\frac{1}{4}$ level tsp) chilli
  powder**
**1 large cooking apple, peeled,
  cored and cut in chunks**
1.1 litres (2 pints) chicken stock
salt and freshly ground pepper
25 ml (5 level tsp) cornflour
**lemon slices and coriander to
  garnish**

1

Fit the metal blade and chop the
carrots, onion and garlic. Heat the
oil in a saucepan, add the
chopped vegetables and fry gently
for 8–10 minutes until soft but
not coloured. Stir in the ground
spices and cook gently for 2
minutes, stirring.

2

Still using the metal blade, chop
the apple finely and add to the
saucepan with the stock. Bring to
the boil, cover and simmer for 40–
45 minutes, until the vegetables
are really soft and the flavours
are well blended.

3

Allow the soup to cool slightly,
then purée it half at a time using a
pulse action. Sieve the soup into
the rinsed out saucepan and
discard the pulp. Add salt and
pepper to taste if necessary.

4

In a small bowl, blend the
cornflour to a smooth paste with
45 ml (3 tbsp) cold water then stir
it into the soup. Bring to the boil,
stirring occasionally. Garnish with
lemon and fresh coriander.

Serves 6

French onion soup

SLICING DISC
GRATING DISC (OPTIONAL)

225 g (8 oz) onions, skinned
**50 g (2 oz) butter or block
  margarine**
30 ml (2 level tbsp) flour
900 ml (1$\frac{1}{2}$ pints) beef stock
salt and freshly ground pepper
bay leaf
French bread
Gruyère cheese

1

Fit the slicing disc and slice the
onions. Melt the butter in a large
saucepan and fry the onions
quickly for 5–10 minutes, until
lightly browned.

2

Stir in the flour and cook, stirring,
for 1–2 minutes. Pour in the stock
gradually. Season, add the bay leaf
and bring to the boil. Cover and
simmer for 30 minutes.

3

Cut the French loaf into diagonal
slices about 1 cm ($\frac{1}{2}$ inch) thick.
Toast them lightly on both sides.
Using the food processor, slice the
cheese, or change to the grating
disc and grate it.

4

Ladle the soup into individual
ovenproof soup bowls, removing
the bay leaf. Place a slice of
toasted French bread in each bowl
to float on top of the soup. Cover

each slice with a slice of Gruyère cheese, or with a thick layer of grated cheese. Stand the bowls on a baking sheet or in a roasting tin and put in the hot oven or under the grill until the cheese is melted.

Serves 4

Mediterranean fish soup with aïoli

METAL BLADE
WHISK (OPTIONAL)

700 g (1½ lb) white fish fillets eg. cod, haddock, whiting, halibut
1 small onion, skinned and quartered
15 ml (1 tbsp) lemon juice
bouquet garni
salt and freshly ground pepper

Aïoli
4 garlic cloves, skinned
3 egg yolks
30 ml (2 tbsp) white wine vinegar
salt and freshly ground pepper
450 ml (¾ pint) olive oil

1

Cut the fish fillets in small strips and place in a saucepan.

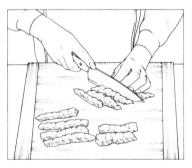

2

Fit the metal blade and chop the onion. Add to the fish with the lemon juice, bouquet garni, seasoning and cold water to cover. Bring to the boil, cover and simmer for 10 minutes or until the fish flakes when tested with a fork.

3

Meanwhile make the aïoli. With the metal blade, chop the garlic very finely. With the metal blade or whisk, put the egg yolks, vinegar and seasoning in the bowl and mix well. Add the oil very gradually through the feeder tube, mixing continuously until the aïoli is smooth and thick.

4

When the fish is cooked remove it from the saucepan with a slotted spoon and keep hot. Strain the cooking liquid, measure off 600 ml (1 pint) and let it cool a little.

5

Spoon off 120 ml (8 tbsp) aïoli and set aside then, with the machine running at slow speed, gradually add the fish liquid to the aïoli remaining in the bowl, through the feeder tube.

6

When it is well mixed, return the soup to the saucepan and cook gently, stirring continuously, for 10 minutes, until thick and creamy. Do not let it boil.

7

Serve the fish and soup separately, with French bread and the remaining aïoli.

Serves 4

Iced cucumber mint soup

METAL BLADE
GRATING DISC

2 large sprigs of fresh mint
1 garlic clove, skinned
1 large cucumber, washed
284 ml (10 oz) natural yogurt
salt and white pepper
mint leaves to garnish

1

Fit the metal blade and chop the mint and garlic finely.

2

Remove the blade, fit the grating disc and grate the cucumber

3

Turn the mixture into a serving bowl and stir in the yogurt and seasoning. Cover and chill.

4

Serve in a tureen, garnished with mint leaves.

Serves 4

Lettuce soup

METAL BLADE

125 g (4 oz) spring onions, trimmed
50 g (2 oz) butter or block margarine
350 g (12 oz) lettuce leaves
15 ml (1 level tbsp) flour
600 ml (1 pint) chicken stock
150 ml ($\frac{1}{4}$ pint) milk
salt and freshly ground pepper

1

Fit the metal blade and chop the spring onions. Melt the butter in a deep saucepan and add the onions. Wash the lettuce under running water and dry with paper towelling. Chop the lettuce in the food processor and add to the onions in the pan.

2

Sauté the onions and lettuce until very soft. Stir in the flour and then add the stock. Bring to the boil, cover and simmer for 45 minutes–1 hour.

3

Allow it to cool slightly. With the metal blade, purée the soup half at a time, using a pulse action.

4

Return it to the saucepan and add the milk and seasonings. Reheat to serving temperature.

Serves 4

Lettuce soup

In country lore, lettuce is said to have a calming effect on the nerves, and modern science—for once at least—has proved country lore right. The dried juices from certain species of lettuce are used in drug manufacture, and all lettuce (in addition to smelling like opium) has a mildly narcotic effect. Large amounts of bolted lettuce stems would have to be eaten before this was readily discernible, though. In normal amounts, such as in this delicate and pretty soup, lettuce is at most calming and sedative. Try using cos lettuce here; it gives a better flavour than most other varieties.

CURRIED CARROT SOUP
PAGE 32

SEAFOOD GUMBO
PAGE 41

Crème vichyssoise

SLICING DISC
METAL BLADE

4 leeks, trimmed and cleaned
1 onion, skinned
50 g (2 oz) butter or block margarine
2 potatoes, peeled
1 litre (1¾ pints) chicken stock
salt and freshly ground pepper
200 ml (7 fl oz) single cream
snipped chives to garnish

1

Fit the slicing disc and slice the leeks and onion. Melt the butter in a saucepan and lightly fry the leeks and onion for about 10 minutes, until they are soft but not coloured.

2

Meanwhile thinly slice the potatoes. Add the stock and potatoes to the soup. Season, cover and cook until the vegetables are soft.

3

Allow the soup to cool a little then fit the metal blade and purée it half at a time, using a pulse action. Turn it into a bowl, stir in 175 ml (6 fl oz) of the cream, with more seasoning if necessary, and chill. Swirl in the remaining cream and sprinkle with snipped chives before serving.

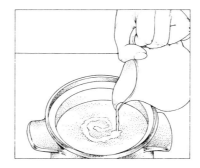

Serves 4

Crème vichyssoise

One might be forgiven for thinking that this delicious chilled soup is as French as Vichy itself, with its water, cooked carrots, and unhappy wartime associations. In fact it was invented in the heart of New York in 1917. Invented by a Frenchman, though—Louis Diat—and he was probably thinking of France at the time, as it is a soup based on the classic combination of leeks and potatoes, known for centuries to every great chef's mother as *potage bonne femme.*

Walnut and mushroom soup

METAL BLADE

350 g (12 oz) button mushrooms
1 small onion, skinned and quartered
50 g (2 oz) butter
15 ml (1 level tbsp) flour
450 ml (¾ pint) chicken stock
450 ml (¾ pint) milk
50 g (2 oz) walnuts
2.5 ml (½ level tsp) salt
freshly ground pepper
150 ml (5 fl oz) cream
finely sliced mushrooms

1

Fit the metal blade. Wipe and chop the mushrooms, set aside. Chop the onion finely. Set aside. Chop the walnuts. Set aside.

2

Melt the butter in a saucepan and fry the onions until soft. Add the chopped mushrooms to the onions and fry for 2 minutes. Remove from the heat, stir in the flour, stock, milk, walnuts and seasoning. Bring to the boil. Simmer, covered, for 30 minutes.

3

Purée the soup using a pulse action, add the finely sliced mushrooms and cream, return to the pan and cook slowly for a further 5 minutes. Serve hot.

Serves 6

Shropshire pea and ham soup

METAL BLADE

1 small onion, skinned and quartered
50 g (2 oz) butter or block margarine
900 g (2 lb) fresh peas, shelled, or 450 g (1 lb) frozen peas
1.1 litres (2 pints) ham stock
2.5 ml ($\frac{1}{2}$ level tsp) caster sugar
2 large sprigs of fresh mint
salt and freshly ground pepper
2 egg yolks
150 ml (5 fl oz) double cream
sprig of fresh mint to garnish

1

Fit the metal blade and chop the onion. Melt the butter in a large saucepan, add the onion and fry gently for 5 minutes.

2

Add the peas, stock, sugar and sprigs of mint. Bring to the boil, cover the pan and simmer for about 30 minutes.

3

Remove the mint sprigs and allow the soup to cool slightly. Then, still using the metal blade, purée the soup half at a time, using a pulse action. Return it to the pan and season to taste; check before you add salt, it may not need any.

4

In the food processor, beat together the egg yolks and cream until just mixed. Add a little soup through the feeder tube and mix again. Pour the cream mixture into the soup and heat gently, stirring; do not boil or it will curdle. Pour into a warmed soup tureen and garnish with a fresh sprig of mint.

Serves 6

Iced tomato soup with fresh basil

METAL BLADE

25 g (1 oz) white bread, crusts removed
450 g (1 lb) ripe tomatoes, skinned and halved
1 medium onion, skinned and quartered
20 ml (4 level tsp) tomato purée
411-g (14$\frac{1}{2}$-oz) can chicken consommé
6 leaves fresh basil
fresh basil to garnish

1

Fit the metal blade. Cut the bread into cubes by hand then chop to breadcrumbs in the food processor. Transfer to a large bowl and set aside.

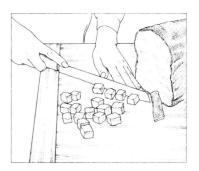

2

With the metal blade still fitted, put the tomatoes, onion, tomato purée, consommé and basil leaves in the food processor. Chop to a smooth purée, using a pulse action. Pour into the bowl with the

breadcrumbs and stir well. Cover
and chill well.

3

To serve, spoon the soup into
individual dishes and garnish with
the basil.

Serves 4

Goulash soup

METAL BLADE

700 g (1½ lb) lean chuck steak
salt and freshly ground pepper
225 g (8 oz) onions, skinned
    and quartered
2 small green peppers, seeded
    and quartered
25 g (1 oz) butter or margarine
4 tomatoes, skinned and
    quartered
141-g (5-oz) can tomato purée
600 ml (1 pint) beef stock
15 ml (1 level tbsp) paprika
450 g (1 lb) potatoes, peeled
142 ml (5 fl oz) soured cream
parsley, to garnish (optional)

1

Wipe the meat with a damp cloth,
remove any excess fat or gristle
and cut the meat into small
pieces. Season well. Fit the metal
blade and chop the onions and
peppers finely.

2

Melt the butter in a large
saucepan, add the onions and
green peppers and fry gently until
tender. Add the meat pieces,
tomatoes, tomato purée, stock
and paprika. Stir well and bring to
the boil. Reduce the heat, cover
and simmer for 2½ hours, stirring
occasionally.

3

Half an hour before the end of
cooking, cut the potatoes into
bite-sized pieces, bring to the boil
in salted water and simmer until
cooked. Drain well and add to the

soup. Check the seasoning and stir
in 30 ml (2 tbsp) soured cream.

4

If you wish, fit the metal blade and
chop the parsley to garnish the
soup. Serve the remaining soured
cream separately, for each person
to spoon into his own soup.

Serves 4

Goulash soup

The Hungarians are great
soup lovers, and authentic
Hungarian goulash—
bográcsgulyás—is *always* a
soup, albeit so filling it's
generally a meal as well.
Magyars in bygone times used
to prepare cauldrons of
spiced, fatty meat soups
which they'd simmer until all
the water had evaporated,
before putting the meat out
into the sun until it dried
hard—and then off they'd go
to war and pillage, with what
must have been one of the
earliest convenience foods,
needing only water and a
pot—strapped in bags to their
saddles.

   Remember that the all-
important paprika comes in
two grades—sweet and hot. If
it's available, use some of
both, the exact proportions of
each depending on your
taste. Doorsteps of bread are
the authentic
accompaniment.

Crab bisque

METAL BLADE

**1 cooked crab, weighing about
   700 g (1½ lb)**
½ small onion, skinned
**1 small carrot, peeled and cut
   in chunks**
50 g (2 oz) butter
1.1 litres (2 pints) fish stock
75 ml (3 fl oz) dry white wine
bouquet garni
50 g (2 oz) long grain rice
salt and freshly ground pepper
**15 ml (1 level tbsp) tomato
   purée**
150 ml (5 fl oz) double cream
juice of 1 lemon

1

Remove the meat from the crab
and set aside. Rinse the shell
thoroughly. Fit the metal blade
and chop the onion and carrot.

2

Melt the butter in a saucepan, add
the chopped vegetables and cook
gently for about 5 minutes until
soft. Add the crab shell, stock,
wine, bouquet garni, rice and salt
and pepper. Bring to the boil,
cover and simmer for about 20
minutes, until the rice is really soft.

3

Remove the crab shell and
bouquet garni and let the liquid
cool a little. Reserve the claw meat
for garnishing and purée the dark
meat with the liquid and tomato
purée, half at a time in the food
processor, using a pulse action.

4

Sieve the soup and return it to the
saucepan, add the cream and
reheat gently. Add lemon juice to
taste and adjust the seasoning.
Garnish each portion with a little
claw meat.

Serves 6

Gazpacho

METAL BLADE

1 garlic clove, skinned
600 ml (1 pint) tomato juice
45 ml (3 tbsp) olive oil
45 ml (3 tbsp) wine vinegar
**30 ml (2 level tbsp) tomato
   purée**
**1 medium cucumber, washed
   and cut into 2.5-cm (1-inch)
   chunks**
**450 g (1 lb) fully ripened
   tomatoes, skinned and
   halved**
**1 small green pepper, seeded
   and quartered**
**1 small onion, skinned and
   quartered**
salt and freshly ground pepper

To garnish
**1 small green pepper, seeded
   and quartered**
ice cubes
3 slices of bread, cubed
50 g (2 oz) butter

1

Fit the metal blade and chop the
garlic finely. Place the tomato
juice, oil, vinegar and tomato
purée in a jug.

2

Place half the vegetables in the
food processor bowl and, using a
pulse action, chop finely. Pour half
the tomato juice mixture in
through the feeder tube while
chopping. Turn into a serving
bowl. Repeat with the remaining
ingredients. Season with salt and
pepper and chill before serving.

3

To prepare the garnish, fit the metal blade and chop the green pepper finely. Gently sauté the bread cubes in the butter until golden brown.

4

To serve, add ice cubes to the soup and garnish with the chopped pepper and croûtons.

Serves 4–6

Seafood gumbo

METAL BLADE
SLICING DISC

450 g (1 lb) peeled prawns
225 g (8 oz) crab meat
225 g (8 oz) scallops
2 garlic cloves, skinned
1 large onion, skinned and
    quartered
50 g (2 oz) streaky bacon,
    rinded and cut up
15 ml (1 level tbsp) flour
2 tomatoes, skinned
bay leaf
1.1 litres (2 pints) fish stock,
    chicken stock or water
175 g (6 oz) long grain rice
225 g (8 oz) okra, trimmed
125 g (4 oz) cooked ham, diced
salt and freshly ground pepper
dash of Tabasco sauce
dash of Worcestershire sauce
fresh parsley to garnish

1

If the prawns, crab meat and scallops are frozen, thaw them and drain thoroughly.

2

Fit the metal blade and chop the garlic finely. Add the onion and chop finely.

3

In a large saucepan cook the bacon gently in its own fat until transparent. Add the onion and garlic and sauté for 10 minutes until lightly golden. Sprinkle in the flour, stir well and cook for 1–2 minutes. Remove from the heat.

4

With the metal blade, chop the tomatoes. Add to the pan with the bay leaf and stock or water. Stir well and bring to the boil. Cover and simmer for 20 minutes. Add the rice and cook for a further 8–10 minutes.

5

Fit the slicing disc and slice the okra. Stir into the pan with the prawns, crab meat, scallops, diced ham and season with salt, pepper, Tabasco and Worcestershire sauces to taste. Simmer for 5 minutes or until hot through.

6

With the metal blade, chop the parsley. Ladle the gumbo into bowls and serve sprinkled with chopped parsley.

Serves 8–10

CHICKEN AND POULTRY

Poussins with apricot stuffing

METAL BLADE

**two 450–700 g (1–1½ lb) oven-
ready poussins**
**50 g (2 oz) butter or block
margarine, melted**

For the stuffing
75 g (3 oz) dried apricots
25 g (1 oz) sultanas
**75 g (3 oz) white bread, crusts
removed**
25 g (1 oz) shelled walnuts
**1.25 ml (¼ level tsp) ground
mixed spice**
salt and freshly ground pepper
15 ml (1 tbsp) lemon juice
**5 ml (1 level tsp) grated lemon
rind**
**25 g (1 oz) butter or block
margarine, melted**
1 egg beaten

For the glaze
**30 ml (2 tbsp) golden syrup or
clear honey**
10 ml (2 tsp) medium sherry

1

Soak the apricots and sultanas in
cold water to cover for
8 hours or overnight.

2

Place the poussins breast side up
on a rack in a roasting tin and
brush with melted butter. Roast in
the oven at 190°C (375°F) mark 5
for about 1½ hours or until cooked,
basting occasionally.

3

To make the stuffing, drain the
apricots and sultanas. Fit the metal
blade and chop the fruit finely.
Remove to a large bowl and set
aside.

4

Cut the bread in chunks, chop to
fine crumbs and add to the
chopped fruit. Chop the walnuts
and add to the fruit. Stir in the
remaining stuffing ingredients and
bind with the egg.

5

Spread the stuffing evenly in a
small ovenproof dish and bake
alongside the poussins for the last
30 minutes of the roasting time.

6

To make the glaze, mix together
the syrup or honey and sherry.
Ten minutes before the end of the
cooking time brush the mixture
over the poussins to glaze them.
Finish roasting the poussins and
serve on a heated serving dish
with the stuffing.

Serves 4

Avocado chicken

METAL BLADE
GRATING DISC

4 chicken breasts, skinned
1 onion, skinned and chopped
150 ml (¼ pint) chicken stock
2 avocados
150 ml (5 fl oz) double cream
juice of 1 lemon
few drops of Tabasco sauce
salt and freshly ground pepper
5-cm (2-inch) piece cucumber

1

Place the chicken breasts in a
roasting tin. Sprinkle with onion
and pour stock around the
chicken. Cover with foil and bake
in the oven at 190°C (375°F)
mark 5, for about 45 minutes until
tender. Leave until cold.

2

Half an hour before serving, fit the
metal blade. Halve the avocados,
remove the stone and scoop out
the flesh with a spoon into the
bowl. Mix until smooth. Add the
remaining ingredients and mix
well. Spoon the sauce over the
chicken breasts.

3

Fit the grating disc and grate the
cucumber. Place a line of grated
cucumber down the centre of
each chicken breast. Serve with
rice if liked.

Serves 4

Roast chicken with almond and apple stuffing

METAL BLADE

1.8-kg (4-lb) oven-ready chicken
25 g (1 oz) butter, melted

For the stuffing
1 small onion, skinned and quartered
1 stick celery, trimmed and cut in chunks
2 eating apples, peeled, cored and quartered
50 g (2 oz) blanched almonds
75 g (3 oz) white bread, crusts removed
50 g (2 oz) butter or block margarine
salt and freshly ground pepper
5 ml (1 level tsp) grated lemon rind
2.5 ml ($\frac{1}{2}$ level tsp) ground coriander
2.5 ml ($\frac{1}{2}$ level tsp) dried thyme
1.25 ml ($\frac{1}{4}$ level tsp) dried marjoram
2.5 ml ($\frac{1}{2}$ level tsp) grated nutmeg

1

Fit the metal blade and chop the onion; remove and set aside. Chop the celery and apple; remove and set aside. Chop the almonds coarsely; remove and set aside. Cut the bread in chunks then chop to fine crumbs.

2

Melt the butter in a pan and fry the onion gently until soft but not coloured; add the celery and apple and fry for a few minutes more. Remove from the heat. Stir in the nuts, breadcrumbs and seasonings and mix well.

3

Stuff the chicken with the almond and apple mixture at the neck end and truss it neatly. Weigh the bird. Place in a roasting tin and brush with melted butter.

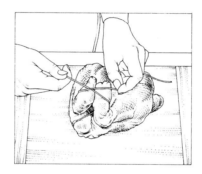

4

Roast the chicken in the oven at 190°C (375°F) mark 5, basting from time to time and allowing 20 minutes per 450 g (1 lb) plus 20 minutes. Put a piece of foil over the breast if it shows signs of becoming too brown.

Serves 6

Chicken puffs

METAL BLADE

225 g (8 oz) cooked chicken, cut in chunks
1 small onion, skinned and quartered
25 g (1 oz) butter or block margarine
25 g (1 oz) flour
150 ml ($\frac{1}{4}$ pint) milk
salt and freshly ground pepper
15 ml (1 tbsp) lemon juice
369-g (13-oz) packet frozen puff pastry, thawed
1 egg, beaten

1

Fit the metal blade and roughly chop the chicken; remove and set aside. Chop the onion finely.

2

Melt the butter in a saucepan and gently fry the onion for 10 minutes, until soft but not coloured. Place the flour and milk in the processor bowl and mix, using a pulse action. Pour on to the onion and bring to the boil, stirring. Season and simmer for 1–2 minutes.

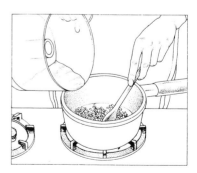

3

Add the chicken and lemon juice. Cover with greaseproof paper and leave to cool.

4

Roll out the pastry and cut out six 15-cm (6-inch) rounds. Divide the chicken mixture between the rounds. Brush the edges with egg, fold in half and seal the edges well.

5

Place on a baking tray and bake in the oven at 200°C (400°F) mark 6 for 15–20 minutes until well risen and golden.

Makes 6

Chicken and lemon croquettes

GRATING DISC
METAL BLADE

50 g (2 oz) Cheddar cheese
bunch of parsley
1 small onion, skinned and quartered
225 g (8 oz) cold cooked chicken
grated rind and juice of 1 lemon
25 g (1 oz) butter or block margarine
25 g (1 oz) flour
150 ml ($\frac{1}{4}$ pint) chicken stock
salt and freshly ground pepper
75 g (3 oz) fresh brown bread, crusts removed
flour for coating
1 egg, beaten
oil for deep frying
sprigs of watercress and lemon slices to garnish

1

Fit the grating disc and grate the cheese; remove and set aside in a bowl. Fit the metal blade and chop the parsley; remove and add 30 ml (2 tbsp) to the cheese. Finely chop the onion, add the chicken and mince, using a pulse action. Mix the chicken and onion into the cheese and parsley and stir in the lemon rind and juice.

2

Melt the butter then put it in the food processor with the flour and stock and mix until smooth. Pour it into a saucepan, bring to the boil and stir until thickened. Season well. Add the sauce to the chicken mixture and mix well. Cool the mixture, cover and place in the refrigerator for 1 hour.

3

Cut the bread in chunks then chop it in the food processor to fine crumbs.

4

Divide the chicken mixture into eight, shape into rolls and coat in flour. Dip the croquettes in the egg and roll them in the breadcrumbs.

5

Heat the oil to 190°C (375°F) and fry a few of the croquettes at a time for 5 minutes until golden brown. Drain on absorbent kitchen paper and keep warm until the remaining croquettes are cooked. Garnish with watercress and lemon.

Serves 4

Chicken and mushrooms au gratin

GRATING DISC
METAL BLADE
SLICING DISC

50 g (2 oz) Parmesan cheese
50 g (2 oz) white bread, crusts removed
350 g (12 oz) cold cooked chicken
125 g (4 oz) mushrooms
600 ml (1 pint) white sauce (see page 95)

1

Fit the fine grating disc and grate the cheese; remove and set aside in a bowl. Cut the bread in chunks. Fit the metal blade and chop it to fine crumbs; remove and add to the cheese.

2

Put the cooked chicken in the food processor and chop roughly, using a pulse action. Fit the slicing disc and slice the mushrooms into the chicken.

3

Stir the chicken mixture into the white sauce and spoon into a buttered gratin dish. Mix together the cheese and breadcrumbs and sprinkle over the top. Bake in the oven at 220°C (425°F) mark 7 for about 20 minutes until bubbling and golden on top.

Serves 4

Soured cream chicken and ham pie

METAL BLADE
SLICING DISC

bunch of parsley
350 g (12 oz) cold cooked chicken, cut in chunks
175 g (6 oz) cooked ham, cut in chunks
1 onion, skinned and quartered
40 g (1½ oz) butter or block margarine
40 g (1½ oz) flour
300 ml (½ pint) chicken stock
150 ml (¼ pint) dry white wine
bay leaf
pinch of grated nutmeg
salt and freshly ground pepper
50 g (2 oz) button mushrooms
2 egg yolks
142 ml (5 fl oz) soured cream
shortcrust pastry made with 225 g (8 oz) plain flour (see page 119)
milk to glaze

1

Fit the metal blade and chop the parsley finely; remove and set aside. Put the chicken and ham in the bowl and chop coarsely; remove and set aside. Put the onion in the bowl and chop.

2

Melt the butter in a saucepan, add the chopped onion and fry gently for 7–8 minutes until the onion is soft but not coloured. Stir in the flour and cook for 1–2 minutes, then gradually stir in the stock and white wine. Bring slowly to the boil, stirring, and simmer for 5 minutes. Remove from the heat and stir in the chicken, ham, 30 ml (2 tbsp) chopped parsley, the bay leaf, nutmeg and salt and pepper to taste.

3

Fit the slicing disc, slice the mushrooms and stir them into the chicken mixture.

4

Fit the metal blade again and mix the egg yolks and soured cream together until smooth. Stir into the chicken and ham mixture and spoon the filling into a 1.1-litre (2-pint) pie dish.

5

Roll out the pastry and use it to cover the pie. Brush with a little milk to glaze. Stand the pie in a roasting tin half-filled with cold water and bake in the oven at 200°C (400°F) mark 6 for 15 minutes, then reduce the temperature to 180°C (350°F) mark 4 and cook for a further 20 minutes or until the pastry is golden brown.

Serves 6

Chicken galantine

METAL BLADE
PLASTIC BLADE
SLICING DISC

1.8-kg (4-lb) oven-ready
  chicken, boned
2 shallots, skinned and halved
225 g (8 oz) pork sausagemeat
225 g (8 oz) lean pork, cut in
  2.5-cm (1-inch) chunks
salt and freshly ground pepper
60 ml (4 tbsp) Madeira
75 g (3 oz) cooked ham, sliced
75 g (3 oz) cooked tongue,
  sliced
50 g (2 oz) bacon fat, sliced
15 g ($\frac{1}{2}$ oz) pistachio nuts,
  blanched
6 black olives, stoned
melted butter
600 ml (1 pint) aspic jelly,
  made with aspic powder
  and chicken stock
5 ml (1 level tsp) gelatine
450 ml ($\frac{3}{4}$ pint) white sauce (see
  page 95)
30–45 ml (2–3 tbsp) double
  cream

For the garnish
$\frac{1}{2}$ cucumber
4 radishes, sliced
few stuffed green olives, sliced
watercress sprigs
radicchio lettuce

1

Lay the boned chicken skin side down on a board and turn the legs and wings inside out.

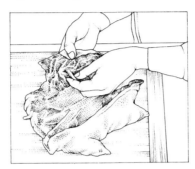

2

Fit the metal blade and chop the shallots. Add the sausagemeat, lean pork, salt and pepper and Madeira and mix until well blended. Spread half the mixture over the chicken.

3

Cut the ham, tongue and bacon fat into long strips 0.5 cm ($\frac{1}{4}$ inch) wide. Lay the nuts, olives and meat strips over the pork mixture.

4

Cover with the remaining pork mixture, draw the sides of the chicken together and sew up, using a trussing needle and string.

5

Place the galantine in a roasting tin, brush with melted butter, season and roast in the oven at 190°C (375°F) mark 5 for $1\frac{3}{4}$ hours.

6

Remove the outside skin and put the galantine on a plate; cover with another plate and weight

down. When completely cold remove the string.

7

Prepare the aspic jelly according to the instructions on the packet. Then dissolve the gelatine in 100 ml (4 fl oz) of the prepared aspic and stir it into the béchamel sauce with the cream. Strain the mixture into the food processor fitted with the plastic blade and mix well together.

8

Put the galantine on a rack in a roasting tin. Coat with the cream sauce and chill well.

9

Fit the slicing disc and slice the cucumber. Garnish the galantine with the sliced vegetables and spoon over the liquid aspic to glaze. Chill the galantine until the aspic is set.

10

Lift the galantine on to a serving plate and arrange the watercress and radicchio around the galantine to garnish.

Serves 6–8

French roast capon with lemon and parsley stuffing

METAL BLADE

3.6-kg (8-lb) oven-ready capon
melted butter
2 rashers bacon, rinded
300 ml ($\frac{1}{2}$ pint) chicken stock

For the stuffing
25 g (1 oz) parsley
200 g (7 oz) white bread, crusts removed
125 g (4 oz) butter
grated rind and juice of 1 small lemon
salt and freshly ground pepper

1

Fit the metal blade and chop the parsley. Cut the bread in chunks, add to the bowl and chop to fine crumbs. Melt the butter in a small saucepan and add to the bowl with the lemon rind and juice, and salt and pepper. Mix lightly.

2

Spoon the stuffing into the neck end of the bird. Truss the capon firmly and weigh the bird.

3

Brush the breast with melted butter and cover with the rashers of bacon. Put the capon in a roasting tin and add the stock.

Roast in the oven at 190°C (375°F) mark 5, basting with stock every 20 minutes, allowing 20 minutes per 450 g (1 lb) plus 20 minutes. Remove the bacon during the last 15 minutes of cooking to brown the breast.

Serves 8–10

Marinated duckling salad

METAL BLADE
WHISK

Two 2.3 kg (5 lb) ducklings
salt and freshly ground pepper
50 g (2 oz) dried apricots, soaked overnight
10 ml (2 tsp) grated horseradish
finely grated rind and juice of 2 oranges
100 ml (4 fl oz) dry white wine
150 ml (5 fl oz) double cream
90 ml (6 tbsp) thick mayonnaise (see page 97)
sprigs of watercress and orange slices to garnish

1

Drain the apricots, place in a saucepan of cold water and bring to the boil. Turn down the heat and simmer for about 20 minutes until just tender. Strain and set aside.

2

Cut away surplus fat from openings, then wipe the ducklings all over with a damp cloth. Pat dry with absorbent kitchen paper. Place side by side on a wire rack over a roasting tin. Prick the birds all over with a sharp skewer and sprinkle generously with salt.

3

Roast in the oven at 180°C (350°F) mark 4 for 1$\frac{3}{4}$ hours or until the birds are really tender. Remove from the oven and leave to cool for about 1 hour.

4

Meanwhile prepare the marinade. Fit the metal blade. Blend together the apricots, horseradish, orange rind and juice and white wine, then set aside.

5

While the ducklings are still warm, strip off the crisp breast skin and reserve. Coarsely shred the flesh, discarding all the remaining skin, fat and bones.

6

Toss the duck meat in the marinade, cover and chill for 3–4 hours or overnight.

7

Once chilled, strain off the marinade and reserve both duck and marinade separately. Fit the whisk. Pour the cream into the bowl and whip lightly, then fold into the mayonnaise. Stir in the reserved marinade, taste and adjust seasoning, then stir in the duck.

8

Snip the reserved duck skin into strips and quickly crisp under a hot grill.

9

To serve, pile the duckling mixture into a serving dish and sprinkle with the duck skin. Garnish with slices of orange and sprigs of watercress.

Serves 8

Roast stuffed duck

METAL BLADE

15 ml (1 tbsp) vegetable oil
duck giblets
600 ml (1 pint) water
1 stick celery, chopped
1 onion, skinned
bay leaf
1.8-kg (4-lb) oven-ready duck
salt and freshly ground pepper
15 ml (1 level tbsp) flour

For the orange and almond stuffing
2 medium onions, skinned and quartered
100 g (4 oz) white bread, crusts removed
25 g (1 oz) butter
10 ml (2 level tsp) dried sage
grated rind and juice of 1 orange
40 g (1½ oz) flaked almonds
salt and freshly ground pepper

1

Heat the oil in a saucepan and brown the gizzard and heart. Add the water, vegetables, bay leaf and liver. Bring to the boil, cover and simmer gently for 45 minutes.

2

Meanwhile make the stuffing. Fit the metal blade and chop the onions. Add the bread in chunks and the sage and chop to fine crumbs. Add the butter, cut in small pieces, the orange rind and juice and plenty of salt and pepper. Mix briefly òn high speed. Add the flaked almonds and

process very briefly to mix.

3

Spoon the stuffing into the neck end and truss. Weigh the duck and calculate the cooking time, at 20 minutes per 450 g (1 lb).

4

Put the duck on a wire rack in a roasting tin and sprinkle the breast liberally with salt and pepper. Rub the seasoning thoroughly into the skin. Prick the skin all over with a sharp fork or skewer to allow the fat to escape. Roast in the oven at 190°C (375°F) mark 5 for the calculated cooking time, basting occasionally with the fat in the tin. When cooked, a skewer pushed into the meat should release clear, not pink, juices. Transfer to a warm plate, remove the trussing strings and keep hot.

5

Strain the giblet stock into a bowl, return it to the pan and bring back to the boil. Boil rapidly until reduced to about 300 ml (½ pint). Cool and skim off the fat.

6

Drain the fat from the roasting tin and tip the remaining juices into the food processor with the flour and reduced stock. Mix until smooth. Pour the gravy into a saucepan and bring to the boil, stirring. Cook for about 10 minutes, stirring, until smooth and thickened. Season to taste and serve with the duck.

Serves 4

Partridge with cabbage

SLICING DISC

2 oven-ready partridges,
   trussed
butter or bacon fat
1 firm cabbage
2 carrots, peeled
1 large onion, skinned
175 g (6 oz) streaky bacon,
   rinded
salt and freshly ground pepper
bouquet garni
chicken stock
2 smoked sausages

1

Fry the partridges in the butter or
bacon fat until golden brown all
over; set aside.

2

Cut the cabbage in quarters,
removing the outside leaves and
any hard pieces of stalk. Fit the
slicing disc and shred the cabbage,
then wash it well. Cook for 2
minutes in boiling salted water,
then drain. Meanwhile, slice the
carrots and onion.

3

Line a casserole with the bacon
and lay half the cabbage over it,
with seasoning to taste. Put the
partridges on top, with the sliced
carrots and onion and bouquet
garni. Add the rest of the cabbage
and more seasoning. Lightly fry
the smoked sausage, cut in half
and place on top.

4

Bring the stock to the boil and add
enough to the casserole to cover
the partridges. Cover and cook in
the oven at 180°C (350°F) mark 4
for 1–1½ hours, or until the birds
are tender.

5

To serve, remove the top layer of
cabbage to a warmed serving dish
and keep it hot. Cut the partridges
into neat joints and the sausages
into pieces and arrange on top of
the cabbage. Spoon the remaining
vegetables round the sides. Spoon
a little of the cooking liquid over.

Serves 4

Roast turkey with chestnut stuffing

METAL BLADE

4.5-kg (10-lb) oven-ready
   turkey
softened dripping or butter

For the stuffing
225 g (8 oz) fresh chestnuts,
   100 g (4 oz) dried chestnuts
   or a 439-g (15½-oz) can
   whole chestnuts
chicken stock
50 g (2 oz) bacon, rinded
100 g (4 oz) fresh white bread,
   crusts removed
sprig of parsley
25 g (1 oz) butter, melted
grated rind of 1 lemon
salt and freshly ground pepper
1 egg, beaten

1

Thaw the turkey completely if
frozen and wipe with a damp
cloth.

2

If using fresh chestnuts, snip the
brown outer skins with scissors or
a sharp knife and place the
chestnuts in a pan of boiling water
for 3–5 minutes. Lift out a few at a
time and peel off both the outer
and inner skins. If using dried
chestnuts, soak overnight in cold
water, drain and pick over to
remove any bits of skin still
clinging to the nuts.

3

Put the fresh or dried chestnuts in a saucepan with chicken stock to cover and simmer for 35–40 minutes, until tender.

4

Meanwhile, fit the metal blade and chop the bacon. Fry it gently in its own fat for 3–5 minutes, until crisp. Drain.

5

Cut the bread in chunks, put it in the food processor and chop to fine crumbs. Add to the bacon. Chop the parsley and add 5 ml (1 tsp) to the bacon and breadcrumbs, discarding the rest.

6

Let the cooked chestnuts cool slightly then tip into the food processor with their cooking liquid or add the can of chestnuts with a little of their liquid. Chop to a smooth purée. Add to the bacon and breadcrumbs with the remaining stuffing ingredients, binding with the beaten egg.

7

Stuff the neck end of the turkey and truss the bird neatly. Spread it with softened dripping or butter. Put it in a roasting tin and roast in the oven at 170°C (325°F) mark 3 for about 3¾–4 hours, basting occasionally. To know if the turkey is cooked, pierce the deepest part of the thigh with a skewer. If the juices are colourless the bird is ready; if not, cook a little longer.

Serves 12

Roast pheasant

METAL BLADE

1 brace oven-ready pheasants
50 g (2 oz) streaky bacon, rinded
50 g (2 oz) butter
30 ml (2 level tbsp) flour
300 ml (½ pint) chicken stock
salt and freshly ground pepper

For the stuffing
½ small onion, skinned
50 g (2 oz) butter, softened
1 cooking apple, peeled and cored
salt and freshly ground pepper

For the garnish
100 g (4 oz) fresh white bread, crusts removed
50 g (2 oz) butter
watercress

1

To make the stuffing, fit the metal blade and chop the onion finely. Heat about 15 g (½ oz) butter and cook the onion until soft. Remove from the heat.

2

Cut the apple up roughly then chop it in the food processor. Add the onion and remaining butter and mix lightly; do not over-process. Use the mixture to stuff the pheasants at the neck end.

3

Truss the birds and cover the breasts with bacon; put them side by side in a roasting tin. Soften the butter and spread it over the legs and wings.

4

Roast in the oven at 230°C (450°F) mark 8 for 10 minutes, then at 200°C (400°F) mark 6 for 15–20 minutes, basting frequently with the butter in the tin.

5

Remove from the oven, discard the bacon and sprinkle the breasts with flour. Baste with butter and cook for a further 15 minutes.

6

Cut the bread in chunks. Fit the metal blade and chop the bread to fine crumbs. Fry the breadcrumbs in butter until they are golden brown, stirring them occasionally to ensure even browning.

7

Put the pheasants on a heated serving dish and remove the trussing strings. Spoon the fried crumbs round the birds, garnish with watercress and keep hot.

8

Skim the fat from the cooking juices. Add the stock and stir to loosen any sediment. Boil for 2–3 minutes and season to taste. Serve the gravy in a sauceboat or jug.

Serves 4

Raised game pie

METAL BLADE
PLASTIC BLADE

100 g (4 oz) lean cooked ham, cut into cubes
175 g (6 oz) lean chuck steak, cut into small cubes
the meat of 1 cooked pheasant or 2 pigeons, cut into small pieces
350 g (12 oz) sausagemeat
salt and freshly ground pepper
beaten egg
300–450 ml ($\frac{1}{2}$–$\frac{3}{4}$ pint) liquid aspic

For hot water crust pastry
350 g (12 oz) plain flour
7.5 ml (1$\frac{1}{2}$ level tsp) salt
75 g (3 oz) lard
200 ml (7 fl oz) water

1

Fit the metal blade, add the ham, steak and pheasant or pigeon meat and roughly chop, using a pulse action.

2

To make the pastry fit the plastic blade. Put the flour and salt in the bowl and mix briefly. Melt the lard in the water, then bring to the boil. With the processor working at slow speed, or using a pulse action, add the liquid through the feeder tube. Gradually increase the speed to maximum and mix to a soft dough. Lightly pinch the dough together with one hand and form into a ball. Cover with cling film and leave to rest for 20–30 minutes for the dough to become elastic and easy to work.

3

Grease a 1.4-litre (2$\frac{1}{2}$-pint) hinged pie mould or an 18-cm (7-inch) loose-bottomed cake tin. Place the mould on a baking sheet. Roll out two-thirds of the pastry on a floured surface to about 0.5 cm ($\frac{1}{4}$ inch) thick. Keep the remaining pastry covered so that it does not harden. Drape the rolled pastry over the rolling pin, lift the pin and unroll the pastry over the tin. Press the pastry into the tin to 0.5 cm ($\frac{1}{4}$ inch) above the rim.

4

Line the base and sides of the pie with sausagemeat, to hold the pastry in a good shape. Mix the ham, steak and pheasant or pigeon meat, season well and fill the pie with the mixture.

5

Roll out the remaining pastry to fit the top of the tin. Brush the pastry edge with water and position the lid over the filling. Pinch the edges together and flute. Brush the lid with beaten egg. Make a hole in the centre for steam to escape.

6

Bake in the oven at 220°C (425°F) mark 7 for 15–20 minutes, reduce the oven temperature to 180°C (350°F) mark 4 and bake for a further 1 hour. Remove the pie from the tin, brush the top and sides with beaten egg and cook for a further 30 minutes or until the meat is tender when tested with a skewer. If the top of the pie appears to be over-browning, cover it with a piece of dampened, crumpled greaseproof paper moulded round the top of the pie.

7

Remove the pie from the oven and cool. Pour the cold but liquid aspic through the hole in the top and leave the pie to get cold. Top up with more aspic if necessary.

Serves 10

POUSSINS WITH APRICOT STUFFING
PAGE 43

TUNA LOAF WITH CUCUMBER SAUCE
PAGE 60

FISH AND SHELLFISH

Crab Imperial

Prawn Cakes

Quenelles in Cream Sauce

Tarragon Fish Pie

Trout with Almond and Lemon Stuffing

Deep Fried Fish Fillets

Tuna Loaf with Cucumber Sauce

Crab imperial

METAL BLADE

450 g (1 lb) crab meat, flaked
1 small green pepper, seeded
   and quartered
25 g (1 oz) butter or block
   margarine
25 g (1 oz) flour
5 ml (1 level tsp) dry mustard
2.5 ml ($\frac{1}{2}$ tsp) Worcestershire
   sauce
pinch of paprika
salt and freshly ground pepper
450 ml ($\frac{3}{4}$ pint) milk
30 ml (2 tbsp) lemon juice
1 egg, beaten

1

If using frozen crab meat, thaw it and drain well. Fit the metal blade and chop the green pepper. Melt the butter in a small frying pan and sauté the pepper gently for about 5 minutes until tender.

2

Drain the fat from the pan into the bowl and add the flour, mustard, Worcestershire sauce, paprika, seasonings and milk. Mix, starting on slow speed and increasing to maximum or using a pulse action, until smooth. Pour into a saucepan and cook gently until the mixture thickens and boils, stirring all the time. Cook for 5 minutes, stirring occasionally, then remove from the heat and stir in the lemon juice.

3

Allow to cool a little then pour a little of the sauce into the food processor. At slow speed, or using a pulse action, gradually add the beaten egg. When well blended, gradually add the remaining sauce through the feeder tube. Stir in the crab meat and green pepper and mix well.

4

Grease a 900-ml (1$\frac{1}{2}$-pint) casserole and spoon in the mixture.
Bake in the oven at 180°C (350°F) mark 4 for 1 hour or until golden.

Serves 4

Prawn cakes

METAL BLADE

450 g (1 lb) shelled prawns
15 g ($\frac{1}{2}$ oz) fresh parsley
25 g (1 oz) white bread, crusts
   removed
30 ml (2 tbsp) mayonnaise (see
   page 97)
5 ml (1 tsp) Worcestershire
   sauce
2.5 ml ($\frac{1}{2}$ level tsp) dry mustard
salt and freshly ground pepper
1 egg
40 g (1$\frac{1}{2}$ oz) butter or block
   margarine
tartare sauce (see page 99)
   and lemon wedges to serve

1

If using frozen prawns thaw and drain well. Fit the metal blade and chop the parsley. Cut the bread in chunks then chop to fine crumbs. Add the prawns and chop roughly, using a pulse action. Add the mayonnaise, seasonings and egg. Mix for a few seconds, using a pulse action. Take care not to turn the mixture to a paste.

2

Divide the mixture into nine portions. Melt the butter in a large frying pan, spoon in the nine portions and flatten them into cakes. Fry them until golden on each side.

3

Serve with tartare sauce and lemon wedges.

Serves 3

Quenelles with cream sauce

METAL BLADE
GRATING DISC

450 g (1 lb) white fish fillets, eg. cod, haddock or hake
100 g (4 oz) white bread, crusts removed
milk
2 egg whites
salt and freshly ground pepper
300 ml (10 fl oz) double cream
100 g (4 oz) Gruyère or Emmental cheese

For the sauce
300 ml ($\frac{1}{2}$ pint) milk
25 g (1 oz) butter
45 ml (3 level tbsp) flour
200 ml (7 fl oz) double cream
100 ml (4 fl oz) dry white wine
5 ml (1 tsp) lemon juice
salt and freshly ground pepper

1

Skin the fish and cut into chunks. Fit the metal blade and mince the fish finely. Soak the bread in a little milk then squeeze out the milk. Add the bread to the fish with the egg whites, salt and pepper and mix well. Gradually add the cream through the feeder tube, mixing lightly. Chill the mixture in the refrigerator for 1 hour.

2

Fit the grating disc and grate the cheese. Set aside.

3

To make the sauce, pour the milk into a saucepan and bring to the boil. Remove from the heat. Fit the metal blade and place the butter and flour in the bowl. Mix until well blended then pour in the hot milk, cream, wine and lemon juice and mix, using a pulse action, until smooth. Pour into the saucepan and bring to the boil, stirring. Season and simmer for 5 minutes, stirring occasionally, until the sauce has thickened.

4

Half fill a large frying pan with water and heat to simmering point. Using two wetted tablespoons, shape the fish mixture into egg-shaped or oval pieces.

5

Spoon the quenelles, several at a time, gently into the water and simmer uncovered for 10 minutes, basting well. When the quenelles are swollen and just set, lift out with a slotted spoon and drain on absorbent kitchen paper. Continue until all the mixture is cooked.

6

Arrange the drained quenelles in a warm flameproof dish large enough to take them in a single layer. Spoon the hot sauce over the quenelles. Sprinkle the grated cheese on top and grill under high heat until melted and golden.

Serves 4–6

Quenelles with cream sauce

Quenelles are little dumplings made of a forcemeat of fish or meat bound together with eggs. They are poached and served with a complimentary sauce. The most famous of all are the *quenelles de brochet*—pike quenelles—but unless you have a fisherman in the family, the raw materials can be hard to come by. The preparation of quenelles is a matter of fearful effort when done without a food processor: they are a good example of the new vistas opened up to the less expert or less energetic cook by modern electrical kitchen equipment.

Tarragon fish pie

METAL BLADE

450 g (1 lb) cod fillet
about 568 ml (1 pint) milk
1 small onion, skinned and
    quartered
50 g (2 oz) butter or block
    margarine
50 g (2 oz) plain flour
salt and freshly ground pepper
4 eggs, hard-boiled and shelled
2 sprigs of fresh tarragon,
    chopped
shortcrust pastry made with
    350 g (12 oz) plain flour (see
    page 119)
beaten egg to glaze

1

Poach the fish in enough milk to cover for about 15 minutes until tender. Drain the fish, reserving the cooking liquid, remove the skin and bones and flake the flesh. Make up the liquid to 600 ml (1 pint) with more milk.

2

Fit the metal blade and chop the onion. Melt the butter in a saucepan and fry the onion gently for 15 minutes.

3

Place the butter and flour in the bowl and mix until well blended. Pour in the milk and mix, using a pulse action, until smooth. Transfer the milk and flour mixture to a saucepan and bring to the boil, stirring. Season and simmer for 5 minutes, stirring occasionally,

until sauce has thickened. Remove from the heat.

4

With the metal blade, chop the eggs roughly and stir into the sauce with the fish and 15 ml (1 tbsp) chopped tarragon.

5

Roll out two-thirds of the pastry and use to line a 23-cm (9-inch) pie dish. Spoon the filling into the lined pie dish. Roll out the remaining pastry for a lid. Brush the pastry edges with beaten egg and cover with the lid, sealing the edges well. Trim and use the pastry trimmings to decorate the top. Brush with egg to glaze and make a hole in the centre to allow steam to escape. Bake in the oven at 200°C (400°F) mark 6 for 40 minutes until golden brown.

Serves 6

Trout with almond and lemon stuffing

METAL BLADE

15 g ($\frac{1}{2}$ oz) blanched almonds
50 g (2 oz) fresh white bread,
    crusts removed
small bunch of fresh parsley
grated rind and juice of $\frac{1}{2}$ small
    lemon
1 egg
2 medium trout, cleaned
150 ml ($\frac{1}{4}$ pint) dry white wine
2.5 ml ($\frac{1}{2}$ level tsp) dried
    tarragon
25 g (1 oz) flaked almonds
15 g ($\frac{1}{2}$ oz) butter
lemon wedges and watercress
    to garnish

1

Fit the metal blade and roughly chop the almonds; remove and set aside. Cut the bread into chunks. Put it in the bowl with the parsley and chop to fine crumbs. Add the lemon rind and juice, egg and chopped almonds and mix lightly.

2

Wash the trout and place in a shallow ovenproof dish.

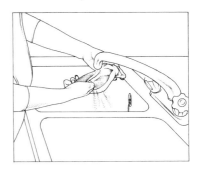

3

Evenly fill the cavities of the fish with the almond and lemon mixture. Mix the white wine and dried tarragon together and pour over the fish. Fry the flaked almonds in the butter until golden brown and spoon over the fish.

4

Cover with foil and cook in the oven at 180°C (350°F) mark 4 for 25 minutes. Remove the foil and cook for a further 5 minutes. Garnish with lemon wedges and watercress.

Serves 4

Trout with almond and lemon stuffing

The ever-popular trout is in fact not one but a whole family of fish, ranging from the very fine Sea or Brown Trout ('Brown' when it's caught in streams and rivers, 'Sea' after it's been to sea and its flesh has turned pink), through the more commonly-flavoured Rainbow Trout (the trout most often farmed, sometimes acquiring pink flesh, though sadly no extra flavour, thanks to its feed), to the rarer Arctic Char, either fished from Arctic waters or from cold lakes like Lake Windermere or Lac Leman. All are good in this recipe, though the better are of course best!

Deep fried fish fillets

PLASTIC BLADE

125 g (4 oz) plain flour
pinch of salt
1 egg
150 ml ($\frac{1}{4}$ pint) milk or milk and water
oil or fat for deep frying
700 g (1$\frac{1}{2}$ lb) white fish fillets seasoned flour

1

Fit the plastic blade. Put the flour and salt in the bowl and mix briefly. Add the egg and half the milk or milk and water and mix until smooth, starting on slow speed and increasing to maximum or using a pulse action. Add the remaining liquid and mix again.

2

Heat the oil or fat in a deep pan to 177–188°C (350–370°F). A cube of bread dropped into the oil should brown in 1 minute.

3

When the oil is hot coat each piece of fish with seasoned flour then dip in the batter.

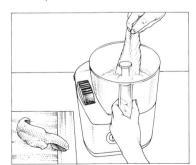

4

Lower the fish gently into the hot oil, cooking two pieces at a time. Cook for 5–10 minutes, until golden.

5

Remove the fish pieces and drain thoroughly on absorbent kitchen paper. Keep hot while you cook the remaining pieces.

Serves 4

Tuna loaf with cucumber sauce

METAL BLADE
SLICING DISC

75 g (3 oz) celery, trimmed
small piece of onion
100 g (4 oz) white bread, crusts
    removed
150 ml ($\frac{1}{4}$ pint) milk
2 eggs
10 ml (2 tsp) tomato purée
two 198-g (7-oz) cans tuna,
    drained
salt and freshly ground pepper

For the sauce
1 cucumber, peeled and
    seeded
25 g (1 oz) butter or block
    margarine
15 ml (1 level tbsp) flour
salt
5 ml (1 tsp) grated lemon rind
10 ml (2 tsp) lemon juice
1 egg yolk

For the garnish
fresh dill weed or parsley
$\frac{1}{2}$ cucumber

1

Grease a 450-g (1-lb) loaf tin. Fit the metal blade and chop the celery and onion finely; remove to a bowl and set aside. Cut the bread in chunks, then chop to fine crumbs. Add the milk, eggs and tomato purée and mix briefly.

2

Flake the tuna with a fork and add with the breadcrumb mixture to the chopped celery and onion. Season with salt and pepper. Stir the mixture well until evenly blended. Pour into the loaf tin.

3

Bake in the oven at 180°C (350°F) mark 4 for 1 hour, or until a knife or skewer inserted in the centre comes out clean. Leave the tuna loaf to cool slightly.

4

Meanwhile make the sauce. Fit the metal blade and chop the cucumber. Put it in a saucepan with water to cover and simmer until just tender. Remove the cucumber, reserve the cooking liquid and make it up to 300 ml ($\frac{1}{2}$ pint) with water.

5

Place the butter and flour in the bowl and mix until well blended. Then pour in the reserved liquid and mix, using a pulse action, until smooth. Pour into a saucepan, add salt, lemon rind and cucumber and bring to the boil, stirring. Simmer for 2–3 minutes, stirring occasionally, until the sauce has thickened. Beat the egg yolk and

stir in a little of the hot sauce. Return the mixture to the pan and stir over gentle heat, without boiling, until the sauce thickens. Loosen the tuna loaf with a spatula and turn it out on to a serving dish.

6

For the garnish chop the dill weed or parsley and remove. Fit the slicing disc and slice the half cucumber. To serve, pour some sauce over the loaf and garnish with the dill or parsley and cucumber slices. Serve the remaining sauce separately.

Serves 4–6

MEAT

Braised Steak

Meat Loaf

Chilli Con Carne

Steak Tartare

Fillet of Beef Wellington

Boeuf en Daube

Moussaka

Spaghetti alla Bolognese

Steak and Kidney Pie

Apricot-stuffed Lamb

Lancashire Hot Pot

Lamb Patties

Lamb Korma

Normandy Pork

Whole Stuffed Cabbage

Pork and Cheddar Croûtes

Country Pork Pie

Stir-fried Pork and Vegetables

Vitello Tonatto

Manicotti with Veal Sauce

Liver Jardinière

Braised steak

SLICING DISC
METAL BLADE

700 g (1½ lb) braising steak
45 ml (3 level tbsp) seasoned
**   flour**
4 medium onions, skinned
50 g (2 oz) fat or oil
1 garlic clove, skinned
1–2 sticks of celery, trimmed
396-g (14-oz) can tomatoes or
**   450 g (1 lb) tomatoes,**
**   skinned and quartered**
15 ml (1 level tbsp) tomato
**   purée**

1

Trim the meat, cut it into 8
portions and beat between sheets
of greaseproof paper to flatten.
Coat with seasoned flour.

2

Fit the slicing disc and slice the
onions. Heat half the fat or oil in a
flameproof casserole and cook the
onions quickly for 5 minutes until
browned; remove from the pan.

3

Add the rest of the fat or oil to the
pan, brown the steak each side for
3 minutes. Reduce the heat.

4

Fit the metal blade and chop the
garlic; then add the celery and
chop. Add them to the pan with
the tomatoes, purée and onions.
Stir, cover and simmer gently for 2
hours or until the meat is tender.

Serves 4

Meat loaf

METAL BLADE

175 g (6 oz) streaky bacon,
**   rinded**
75 g (3 oz) fresh bread, crusts
**   removed**
1 small onion, skinned and
**   quartered**
225 g (8 oz) lean cooked lamb
15 ml (1 level tbsp) tomato
**   purée**
10 ml (2 tsp) chopped fresh
**   sage**
150 ml (¼ pint) milk
1 egg
15 ml (1 tbsp) red wine
salt and freshly ground pepper

1

Lightly grease a 450-g (1-lb) loaf tin.
Stretch the bacon rashers with the
back of a knife and line the tin
with them.

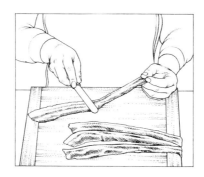

2

Fit the metal blade, cut the bread
in chunks then chop it to fine
breadcrumbs. Add the onion and
chop roughly. Cut the lamb in
chunks and add to the onion with
all the remaining ingredients.
Chop the lamb coarsely, using a
pulse action.

3

Spoon the meat mixture into the
lined loaf tin and press down. Turn
the ends of the bacon rashers over
the top of the meat.

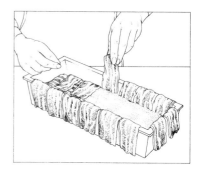

4

Cover the tin with foil and bake in
the oven at 200°C (400°F) mark 6
for 1–1½ hours. Turn out and serve
in slices, hot or cold.

Serves 4

RAISED GAME PIE
PAGE 52

LAMB KORMA
PAGE 72

CHILLI CON CARNE
PAGE 67

STIR-FRIED PORK AND VEGETABLES
PAGE 78

Chilli con carne

METAL BLADE

350 g (12 oz) dried or 432-g
(15¼-oz) can red kidney
beans, drained
1 garlic clove, skinned
1 large onion, skinned and
quartered
1 medium carrot, peeled and
cut in chunks
2 sticks celery, trimmed and
cut in chunks
15 ml (1 tbsp) vegetable oil
700 g (1½ lb) lean stewing steak,
cut in 2.5-cm (1-inch) chunks
396-g (14-oz) can tomatoes
45 ml (3 level tbsp) tomato
purée
15 ml (1 level tbsp) paprika
5 ml (1 level tsp) sugar
5–10 ml (1–2 level tsp) chilli
powder
15 ml (1 tbsp) vinegar
salt and freshly ground pepper
30 ml (2 tbsp) red wine
(optional)

1

If using dried kidney beans, soak
them overnight in cold water.
Drain.

2

Cook the beans in boiling water
for 45 minutes, or until tender.
Add salt for the last 10 minutes
cooking. Drain and rinse under
cold water.

3

Fit the metal blade and chop the
garlic finely. Add the onion, carrot
and celery and chop roughly. Fry
the vegetables in the oil for 5
minutes until softened.

4

With the metal blade, using a
pulse action, mince the beef. Add
the meat to the vegetables and fry
for a further 5 minutes.

5

Add the tomatoes, tomato purée,
paprika, sugar, chilli powder,
vinegar and seasoning and simmer
gently for 30 minutes. Add the
cooked or canned beans and the
wine if used and cook for a further
10 minutes.

6

Serve with a fresh green salad and
hot French bread.

Serves 4–6

Steak tartare

METAL BLADE

2 sprigs fresh parsley
1 onion, skinned and quartered
30 ml (2 tbsp) capers
450 g (1 lb) fillet steak, cubed
salt and freshly ground pepper
10 ml (2 tsp) grated horseradish
a few drops tabasco
4 egg yolks
sprigs of watercress to garnish

1

Fit the metal blade. Chop the
parsley finely, add the onion and
capers and chop finely. Remove
from the bowl and set aside.

2

Put half the meat in the bowl with
the salt, pepper, 5 ml (1 tsp)
horseradish and a couple of drops
of tabasco. Chop until finely
minced. Add to the onion mixture.
Repeat this process using the rest
of the beef, seasoning, horseradish
and tabasco.

3

Mix the onion and beef mixtures
together and divide between four
plates, shaping into neat mounds.

4

Make a hollow in each mound and
drop in a whole egg yolk.

5

Chill in the refrigerator for at least
an hour before serving. Garnish
with sprigs of watercress.

Serves 4

Fillet of beef Wellington

SLICING DISC
METAL BLADE

1.8 kg (4 lb) fillet of beef
freshly ground pepper
100 g (4 oz) butter
225 g (8 oz) button mushrooms
175 g (6 oz) smooth liver pâté
368-g (13-oz) packet frozen
**   puff pastry, thawed**
beaten egg to glaze

1

Trim and tie up the fillet at intervals to retain its shape. Season with pepper.

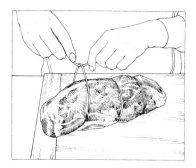

2

Melt 50 g (2 oz) butter in a large frying pan. When foaming, add the meat and fry briskly on all sides. Press down with a wooden spoon while frying to seal the surface well. Roast in the oven at 220°C (425°F) mark 7 for 20 minutes. Cool the beef, chill, and remove the string.

3

Fit the slicing disc and slice the mushrooms. Sauté them in the remaining butter until soft; chill.

4

Fit the metal blade, put the pâté in the bowl and work, starting at slow speed and increasing to maximum or using a pulse action, until really soft and smooth. Add the cooked mushrooms and mix in with a few short bursts.

5

Roll out the pastry to a large rectangle about 33 × 28 cm (13 × 11 inch) and 0.5 cm ($\frac{1}{4}$ inch) thick. Spread the pâté mixture down the centre of the pastry. Place the meat in the centre. Brush the edges of the pastry with egg.

6

Fold the pastry edges over lengthways and turn the pastry over so that the join is underneath. Fold the ends under the meat. Decorate with leaves cut from the pastry trimmings. Chill until the pastry is firm.

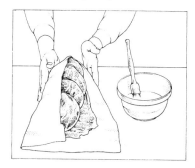

7

Just before baking, brush with egg. Cook in the oven at 220°C (425°F) mark 7 for about 50 minutes, covering with foil halfway through the cooking.

Serves 8

Boeuf en daube

SLICING DISC

1.1-kg (2$\frac{1}{2}$-lb) piece top rump of beef
25 g (1 oz) butter or block margarine
30 ml (2 tbsp) vegetable oil
225 g (8 oz) onions, skinned
450 g (1 lb) carrots, peeled
225 g (8 oz) salt pork, rinded and cubed
300 ml ($\frac{1}{2}$ pint) dry white wine
150 ml ($\frac{1}{4}$ pint) beef stock
5 ml (1 level tsp) dried basil
2.5 ml ($\frac{1}{2}$ level tsp) dried rosemary
bay leaf
2.5 ml ($\frac{1}{2}$ level tsp) ground mixed spice
salt and freshly ground pepper
6 black olives

1

Tie the beef firmly with string. Heat the butter and oil together in a frying pan and fry the meat until it is just browned and sealed all over. Remove it from the pan, drain on absorbent kitchen paper and place it in a casserole.

2

Fit the slicing disc and slice the onions and carrots thinly. Fry the vegetables and salt pork in the fat remaining in the pan until golden brown. Drain well and spoon around the beef.

3

Pour over the wine and stock and stir in the herbs, spice and seasoning. Bring to the boil, cover the casserole and cook in the oven at 170°C (325°F) mark 3 for about 2½ hours. Turn the meat occasionally while cooking.

4

Stone and roughly chop the olives. Stir them into the daube, cover again and cook for a further 30 minutes or until the beef is tender.

5

To serve, remove the meat from the casserole, cut away the string and slice the meat thickly. Skim off the fat from the cooking juices, boil them up again and return the meat slices to the casserole.

Serves 6

Moussaka

SLICING DISC
METAL BLADE
GRATING DISC
PLASTIC BLADE

450 g (1 lb) aubergines
salt and freshly ground pepper
2 large onions, skinned
1 garlic clove, skinned
90 ml (6 tbsp) vegetable oil
700 g (1½ lb) boneless lamb or
  stewing beef
396-g (14-oz) can tomatoes
25 g (1 oz) Parmesan cheese
284 ml (10 oz) natural yogurt
2 eggs
1.25 ml (¼ level tsp) grated
  nutmeg

1

Cut the aubergines in half lengthways. Fit the slicing disc and slice the aubergines. Place the slices in a colander, sprinkling each layer with salt. Cover and leave for 30 minutes.

2

Meanwhile, slice the onions and remove. Fit the metal blade and chop the garlic finely. Fry the onions and garlic in 30 ml (2 tbsp) oil for 5 minutes until golden.

3

Cut the meat into 2.5-cm (1-inch) chunks, put in the food processor and mince finely using a pulse action. Add the meat to the onions and garlic and fry for a further 10 minutes until browned. Add the tomatoes with their juice, season and simmer for 20 minutes.

4

Drain the aubergine slices, rinse and dry well. In a frying pan, cook for 4–5 minutes in the remaining oil, turning once. Add more oil to the pan if necessary.

5

Arrange a layer of aubergine in the bottom of a large ovenproof dish and spoon over a layer of meat. Continue the layers until all the meat and aubergines are used.

6

Fit the fine grating disc and grate the Parmesan; remove and set aside. Fit the plastic blade and beat together the yogurt, eggs, nutmeg and salt and pepper. Through the feeder tube add half the Parmesan and mix again. Pour over the dish and sprinkle with the remaining cheese.

7

Bake in the oven at 180°C (350°F) mark 4 for about 45 minutes until the top is golden.

Serves 6

Spaghetti alla bolognese

METAL BLADE
GRATING DISC

1 garlic clove, skinned
1 medium carrot, peeled and
   cut in chunks
1 medium onion, skinned and
   quartered
30 ml (2 tbsp) vegetable oil
450 g (1 lb) lean stewing beef
225 g (8 oz) streaky bacon,
   rinded
100 g (4 oz) button mushrooms
30 ml (2 level tbsp) flour
226-g (8-oz) can tomatoes
300 ml ($\frac{1}{2}$ pint) beef stock
60 ml (4 level tbsp) tomato
   purée
2.5 ml ($\frac{1}{2}$ level tsp) dried
   oregano
salt and freshly ground pepper
30 ml (2 tbsp) red wine
225 g (8 oz) spaghetti
Parmesan cheese to serve

1

Fit the metal blade and chop the garlic finely. Add the carrot and onion and chop finely. Heat the oil in a large saucepan and fry the chopped vegetables for about 5 minutes until softened.

2

Cut the meat in chunks and put it in the food processor with the bacon. Chop finely, using a pulse action. Add the meats to the pan. Fry for a further 10 minutes until lightly browned.

3

With the metal blade roughly chop the mushrooms. Stir them into the meat mixture with the flour. Chop the tomatoes to a purée and add to the pan with the stock, tomato purée, oregano, seasoning and wine. Bring to the boil, then simmer for 50–60 minutes until the meat is tender.

4

Fit the fine grating disc and grate the Parmesan. Cook the spaghetti in boiling salted water for 12–15 minutes. Drain well. Serve with the sauce poured over and topped with Parmesan cheese.

Serves 4

Steak and kidney pie

METAL BLADE

shortcrust pastry made with
   225 g (8 oz) plain flour (see
   page 119)
1 large onion, skinned and
   quartered
225 g (8 oz) lamb, pig or ox
   kidney
25 g (1 oz) flour
900 g (2 lb) stewing steak, cut
   into 2.5-cm (1-inch) chunks
vegetable oil
100 ml (4 fl oz) red wine
225 ml (8 fl oz) beef stock
10 ml (2 tsp) Worcestershire
   sauce
salt and freshly ground pepper
1 egg yolk, beaten with 5 ml
   (1 tsp) water, to glaze

1

Fit the metal blade and make the shortcrust pastry. Wrap in cling film or foil and chill while you prepare the filling.

2

Chop the onion. Wash the kidney and remove the membrane and hard white core. Cut the kidney into 2.5-cm (1-inch) chunks. Spread the flour on waxed paper. Coat the kidney and steak with it.

3

Heat 45 ml (3 tbsp) oil in a large flameproof casserole or saucepan. Add the pieces of meat to the pan a few at a time and cook until browned all over; remove the pieces as they brown, adding more oil as necessary.

4

When all the meat is browned, reduce the heat and add the onion to the fat remaining in the pan. Cook until it is almost tender, stirring occasionally. Stir in the wine stock, Worcestershire sauce, salt and pepper. Add the browned meat and bring to the boil. Reduce the heat, cover and simmer for 2 hours or until the meat is tender.

5

Spoon the filling into a 1.1-litre (2-pint) pie dish and place a pie funnel in the centre. Roll out the pastry to a circle 5 cm (2 inches) larger all round than the dish. Cut a 2.5-cm (1-inch) strip from the pastry edge and lay on the dampened rim of the dish. Lay the pastry circle on top; trim and flute. Brush the pastry with the egg yolk and water glaze and make a slit in the centre for steam to escape.

6

Bake in the oven at 200°C (400°F) mark 6 for about 40 minutes. Cover loosely with foil if the pastry browns too quickly.

Serves 6

Apricot-stuffed lamb

METAL BLADE

75 g (3 oz) brown bread, crusts removed
sprig of fresh thyme
1 medium onion, skinned and quartered
4 rashers of streaky bacon, rinded and cut up
50 g (2 oz) dried apricots, soaked overnight
salt and freshly ground pepper
1 egg, beaten
1.4-kg (3-lb) loin of lamb, boned
watercress to garnish

1

Cut the bread in chunks. Fit the metal blade, add the bread and thyme and chop until the bread is in fine crumbs. Add the onion, bacon, apricots and seasoning and chop. Add the beaten egg through the feeder tube and mix just enough to bind the mixture.

2

Lay the lamb out flat, fat side down, and spread the cold stuffing over the lamb.

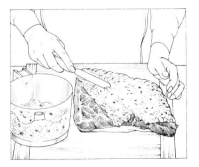

3

Roll up the loin of lamb and tie with string at regular intervals.

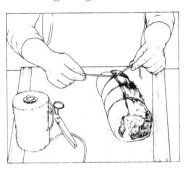

4

Weigh the joint and roast in the oven at 180°C (350°F) mark 4 for 25 minutes per 450 g (1 lb), plus 25 minutes. Serve garnished with watercress sprigs.

Serves 4–6

Lancashire hot-pot

SLICING DISC

225 g (8 oz) onions, skinned
450 g (1 lb) potatoes, peeled
8 middle neck lamb chops
2 lamb's kidneys, skinned and
diced (optional)
salt and freshly ground pepper
300 ml ($\frac{1}{2}$ pint) beef stock
25 g (1 oz) lard or dripping

1

Fit the slicing disc and slice the onions and potatoes.

2

Remove any excess fat from the chops and put them in a casserole. Add the onions, the kidneys if used and lastly the potato; season well. Pour in the stock and brush the top of the potato with the melted lard or dripping.

3

Cover and cook in the oven at 170°C (325°F) mark 3 for 2 hours, or until the meat and potatoes are tender. Remove the lid and brown the top layer of potatoes in the oven at 220°C (425°F) mark 7 for 20 minutes

Note Lancashire hot-pot is traditionally made containing oysters. Allow 1 shelled oyster to each lamb chop, putting the oysters on top of the chops in the casserole.

Serves 4

Lamb patties

METAL BLADE

700 g (1$\frac{1}{2}$ lb) boneless lamb
small bunch of fresh parsley
15 ml (1 level tbsp) grated
lemon rind
15 ml (1 tbsp) lemon juice
small bay leaf, crushed
pinch dried rosemary
salt and freshly ground pepper
6 rashers streaky bacon, rinded

1

Fit the metal blade. Put the lamb, parsley, lemon rind and juice, dried herbs and seasoning in the bowl. Using a pulse action, mince the lamb finely.

2

Shape the mixture into six round patties. Wrap a rasher of bacon round each patty and secure with wooden cocktail sticks.

3

Place the patties on a greased rack in the grill pan and cook under a hot grill for 5 minutes on each side, until well browned.

Serves 6

Lamb korma

SLICING DISC
METAL BLADE

225 g (8 oz) onions, skinned
700 g (1$\frac{1}{2}$ lb) boned shoulder of
lamb
4 garlic cloves, skinned
2.5-cm (1-inch) piece fresh
ginger root, peeled
40 g (1$\frac{1}{2}$ oz) blanched almonds
5 ml (1 level tsp) ground
cardamom
5 ml (1 level tsp) ground cloves
5 ml (1 level tsp) ground
cinnamon
5 ml (1 level tsp) ground cumin
2.5 ml ($\frac{1}{2}$ level tsp) ground
coriander
1.25 ml ($\frac{1}{4}$ level tsp) cayenne
pepper
60 ml (4 tbsp) vegetable oil
284 ml (10 oz) yogurt
salt
toasted flaked almonds to
garnish

1

Fit the slicing disc, slice the onions and set aside. Cut the lamb into 2.5-cm (1-inch) cubes.

2

Fit the metal blade and chop the garlic. Add the ginger and chop. Add the almonds and 60 ml (4 tbsp) cold water and process until it becomes a smooth paste. Add the spices and mix well.

3

Heat the oil in a flameproof casserole and brown the meat a few pieces at a time. Remove the meat from the pan as it browns and set aside. Lower the heat a little, add the onions and fry until lightly browned.

4

Stir the almond paste into the meat. Mix well and cook, stirring, for 3–4 minutes.

5

Return the meat to the pan, add the yogurt and mix well. Add salt to taste.

6

Bring to the boil then reduce to a simmer, cover and cook for about 2–3 hours or until tender, stirring occasionally to prevent sticking. Serve hot garnished with toasted flaked almonds.

Serves 4

Normandy pork

SLICING DISC
METAL BLADE

900 g (2 lb) fillet of pork
30 ml (2 level tbsp) seasoned flour
225 g (8 oz) button mushrooms
300 ml ($\frac{1}{2}$ pint) dry white wine
40 g ($1\frac{1}{2}$ oz) butter
30 ml (2 tbsp) brandy
small bunch of fresh parsley
150 ml (5 fl oz) double cream
salt and freshly ground pepper

1

Cut the pork into pieces about the size and shape of potato chips and toss in the seasoned flour.

2

Fit the slicing disc and slice the mushrooms. Bring the wine to the boil, add the mushrooms and simmer, covered, for 10–15 minutes, until tender.

3

Brown the pork in the hot butter. Warm the brandy in a ladle over a flame, set it alight and when the flames die down, pour it over the meat.

4

Add the mushrooms and wine to the pork and simmer, covered, for 30 minutes, or until the meat is tender. Strain the pork and mushrooms, put in a serving dish and keep warm.

5

Fit the metal blade, chop the parsley and add 30 ml (2 tbsp) with the cream to the juices in the pan; check the seasoning. Simmer without boiling until the sauce thickens and pour it over the pork. Serve with rice and a green salad.

Serves 6

Whole stuffed cabbage

METAL BLADE
SLICING DISC

450 g (1 lb) lean stewing steak
1 garlic clove, skinned
1 onion, skinned and quartered
798-g (28-oz) can tomatoes
salt and freshly ground pepper
141-g (5-oz) can tomato purée
15 ml (1 level tbsp) brown
  sugar
2.5 ml ($\frac{1}{2}$ tsp) Worcestershire
  sauce
pinch ground allspice
1 large cabbage
75 g (3 oz) long grain rice,
  cooked

1

Fit the metal blade and, using a pulse action, mince the beef; remove and set aside. Chop the garlic finely, add the onion, and chop finely; remove and set aside.

2

Put the tomatoes with their liquid, 2.5 ml ($\frac{1}{2}$ level tsp) salt, tomato purée, brown sugar, Worcestershire sauce and allspice into a pan. Bring to the boil, stirring; reduce the heat, cover and simmer for 20 minutes, stirring from time to time.

3

Discard the tough outer leaves from the cabbage. Remove two large leaves and reserve. Cut out the stem and centre of the cabbage, leaving a 2.5-cm (1-inch) thick shell.

4

Discard the hard core, fit the slicing disc and slice the cabbage removed from the middle.

5

Put the beef, onion, garlic, pepper, 5 ml (1 level tsp) salt and 75 g (3 oz) sliced cabbage into a large flameproof casserole and cook for about 15 minutes. Add the rice and 225 ml (8 fl oz) of the tomato sauce and stir to blend well. Remove from the heat.

6

Spoon the beef mixture into the cabbage shell and cover the top with the two large reserved leaves. Tie the cabbage with string to hold the leaves firmly in position.

7

Pour 600 ml (1 pint) water into the pan used for the beef mixture, stirring to loosen the sediment. Add the remaining chopped cabbage and tomato sauce. Stir well. Put the cabbage, stem down, in the sauce. Bring to the boil, reduce the heat, cover and simmer for 2 hours, basting the cabbage with sauce occasionally.

8

To serve, put the cabbage stem down in a heated serving dish. Remove the string. Spoon over the tomato sauce and cut the cabbage into wedges for serving.

Serves 6

Whole stuffed cabbage

Of the many different varieties of cabbage we enjoy, perhaps the finest, and the best for stuffing, is the Savoy cabbage, a winter variety developed in Savoy during the Middle Ages and brought to Britain during the seventeenth century. Most of our cabbage has come to us via Italy, in fact; the Romans were very fond of it, and it was they who first brought it here nearly 2,000 years ago. The name itself is derived from the Latin word for 'head'—*caput*—through its Norman French translation, *caboche*, though what the Romans and Normans thought of as a head we now describe as a heart: 'cabbages' are more correctly *hearting* varieties of the cabbage family.

FILLET OF BEEF WELLINGTON
PAGE 68

SPINACH TIMBALE
PAGE 83

Pork and Cheddar croûtes

GRATING DISC
METAL BLADE

1 pork fillet, about 350 g (12 oz)
25 g (1 oz) mature Cheddar
**   cheese**
25 g (1 oz) slice white bread,
**   crusts removed**
small bunch of fresh parsley
pinch of salt
pinch of cayenne pepper
beaten egg
2 rashers streaky bacon, rinded
shortcrust pastry made with
**   225 g (8 oz) plain flour (see**
**   page 119)**

1

Place the pork fillet between greaseproof paper and beat out as thinly as possible with a meat mallet or rolling pin.

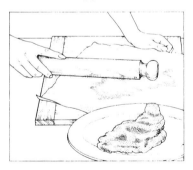

2

Fit the grating disc and grate the cheese; remove and set aside. Cut the bread into chunks. Fit the metal blade and chop the parsley and bread together until the bread makes fine crumbs. Add the salt, cayenne and grated cheese and with the machine on slow speed, or using a pulse action, add just enough beaten egg to bind the mixture lightly together (about ½ an egg).

3

Spread the stuffing over the pork and roll up tightly from the narrow end. Wrap the roll in cling film or foil and chill for 30 minutes.

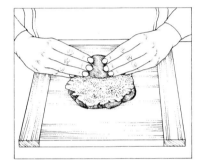

4

Remove from the refrigerator and cut in 4. Stretch the bacon rashers with the back of a knife, halve them and wrap one piece round each roll of pork. Set aside.

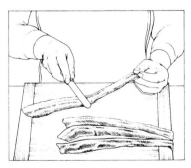

5

Roll out the pastry and cut four 15-cm (6-inch) rounds and four 12.5-cm (5-inch) rounds. Flatten the pork slightly with the heel of your hand. Place a stuffed pork roll in the centre of each of the smaller pastry circles, brush the edges with beaten egg and place the larger pastry circles on top. Seal and flute the edges and bind with egg. Make a hole in the centre of each croûte to allow steam to escape.

6

Place on a baking sheet and bake in the oven at 200°C (400°F) mark 6 for 15 minutes to brown the pastry then reduce to 170°C (325°F) mark 3, cover with foil and cook for a further 30 minutes. Serve hot or cold.

Serves 4

Country pork pie

METAL BLADE

shortcrust pastry made with 525 g (18 oz) plain flour (see page 119)
1 large onion, skinned and quartered
175 g (6 oz) streaky bacon rashers, rinded
700 g (1½ lb) lean pork
350 g (12 oz) sausagemeat
5 ml (1 level tsp) dried sage
10 ml (2 tsp) Worcestershire sauce
salt and freshly ground pepper
4 eggs, hard-boiled and shelled
beaten egg to glaze

1

Roll out two-thirds of the pastry and use to line a 20.5-cm (8-inch) round loose-bottomed cake tin.

2

Fit the metal blade and chop the onion roughly. Add the bacon and pork and mince, using a pulse action. Turn the mixture into another bowl and mix together with the sausagemeat, sage, Worcestershire sauce and salt and pepper.

3

Place half the pork mixture in the lined tin. Arrange the eggs over the top and cover with the remaining pork mixture.

4

Roll out the remaining pastry and make a lid to cover the pie. Dampen the edge and seal and flute. Make a slit in the centre and use any pastry trimmings to decorate the top. Brush with beaten egg to glaze.

5

Bake in the oven at 200°C (400°F) mark 6 for 1½ hours, covering the lid with foil after 30 minutes to prevent burning. Leave in the tin until cold then turn out to serve.

Serves 8–10

Stir-fried pork and vegetables

METAL BLADE
SLICING DISC

1 cm (½ inch) fresh ginger, peeled
60 ml (4 tbsp) soy sauce
15 ml (1 tbsp) dry sherry
12.5 ml (2½ level tsp) cornflour
6.25 ml (1¼ level tsp) sugar
two 350-g (12-oz) pork fillets, thinly sliced
150 ml (¼ pint) vegetable oil
225 g (8 oz) carrots, peeled
225 g (8 oz) courgettes
2 sticks celery, trimmed
125 g (4 oz) mushrooms
salt

1

Fit the metal blade and chop the ginger finely. Mix the ginger with the soy sauce, sherry, cornflour and sugar in a bowl; add the pork and toss well.

2

Fit the slicing disc and slice the carrots; remove and set aside. Slice the courgettes, remove and set aside. Slice the celery, remove and set aside. Finally slice the mushrooms.

3

Heat 60 ml (4 tbsp) oil in a flameproof casserole and add the vegetables and 1.25 ml (¼ level tsp) salt. Fry quickly, stirring, until the vegetables are coated with oil. Continue to stir-fry until the vegetables are tender but still crisp. Place the vegetables on a heated dish and keep hot.

4

Heat the remaining oil in the casserole until very hot. Add the meat mixture and stir-fry for about 2 minutes until the meat is browned. Return the vegetables to the casserole and heat through.

Serves 6

Vitello tonnato

SLICING DISC
METAL BLADE

1 small carrot, peeled
1 onion, skinned
1 stick of celery, trimmed
700 g (1½ lb) boneless leg of veal
4 peppercorns
5 ml (1 level tsp) salt
99-g (3½-oz) can tuna, drained
4 anchovy fillets
150 ml (¼ pint) olive oil
2 egg yolks
pepper
15 ml (1 tbsp) lemon juice
capers and lemon slices to garnish

1

Fit the slicing disc and slice the carrot, onion and celery.

2

Tie the meat into a neat roll and put into a saucepan with the bone, if you have it, carrot, onion, celery, peppercorns, salt and water to cover. Bring to the boil, cover and simmer for about 1 hour until tender. Remove the pan from the heat and leave until cold.

3

Meanwhile fit the metal blade and put the tuna, anchovy fillets, 15 ml (1 tbsp) olive oil, the egg yolks, pepper and lemon juice in the bowl and mix on high speed. Switch to slow speed and add the remaining oil a little at a time

through the feeder tube. Continue mixing until the sauce resembles thin cream.

4

Remove the cold meat from the pan and cut into slices, arrange in a shallow dish and coat completely with the sauce. Cover and leave overnight.

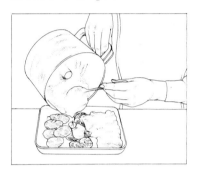

5

Serve cold, with a garnish of capers and lemon slices.

Serves 4–6

Manicotti with veal sauce

METAL BLADE
GRATING DISC

50 g (2 oz) plain flour
2.5 ml ($\frac{1}{2}$ level tsp) salt
2 eggs
15 ml (1 tbsp) vegetable oil
100 ml (4 fl oz) water
oil for frying
225 g (8 oz) lean veal
15 g ($\frac{1}{2}$ oz) butter or block margarine
450 ml ($\frac{3}{4}$ pint) tomato sauce (see page 96)
100 g (4 oz) Mozzarella cheese
15 ml (1 tbsp) grated Parmesan cheese
225 g (8 oz) Ricotta cheese
1 egg
salt and freshly ground pepper

1

Fit the metal blade. Put the flour and salt in the bowl and mix briefly. Add the egg, oil and half the water and mix, starting on slow speed and increasing to maximum or using a pulse action. Add the remaining water through the feeder tube and mix.

2

Brush a small frying pan lightly with oil and place over moderate heat. Pour about 30 ml (2 tbsp) batter into the pan and tip it so that the batter coats the bottom evenly. Cook for about 30 seconds until the underside is brown and the top is set. Remove from the

pan. Repeat with remaining batter.

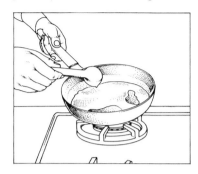

3

To make the sauce mince the veal with the metal blade, using a pulse action. Melt the butter in a large frying pan, add the meat and cook until it is well browned, stirring occasionally. Stir in the tomato sauce. Spoon one-third of the sauce over the base of an ovenproof dish or roasting tin.

4

To make the filling, fit the coarse grating disc and grate the Mozzarella; remove and set aside. Fit the metal blade, add the Ricotta or cottage cheese to the bowl with the Parmesan cheese, eggs and seasoning and mix well.

5

Spread the pancakes out and spoon some of the cheese mixture down the centre of each one. Sprinkle over the grated Mozzarella. Fold the pancake sides over the filling so it is completely enclosed. Arrange seam side down on the sauce in the dish. Spoon the remaining sauce over the top and bake it in the oven at 190°C (375°F) mark 5 for 30 minutes or until hot and bubbling.

Serves 4

Liver jardinière

SLICING DISC

450 g (1 lb) ox liver
30 ml (2 level tbsp) flour
100 g (4 oz) streaky bacon
2 onions, skinned
2 large green peppers, seeded
226-g (8-oz) can tomatoes
salt and freshly ground pepper

1

Slice the liver and lightly coat the slices with flour. Fry the bacon in its own fat until crisp; drain and set aside. Pour off all but 45 ml (3 tbsp) fat from the pan and reserve it.

2

Reheat the fat in the pan. Fry the liver a few pieces at a time until lightly browned on both sides.

3

Fit the slicing disc and slice the onions and green peppers. Add 30 ml (2 tbsp) reserved bacon fat to the pan and lightly brown the onions and green peppers. Drain the juice from the tomatoes and add it to the pan; season.

4

Place the liver on top of the vegetables, cover and cook gently for 25 minutes or until tender. Towards the end of the cooking time, add the tomatoes to heat through. Crumble the reserved bacon on top of the liver to serve.

Serves 4

RICE VEGETABLES AND SALADS

HERRING SALAD

DANISH CUCUMBER SALAD

COLESLAW

WALDORF SALAD

SPINACH TIMBALE

FRENCH BEANS WITH COURGETTES AND BACON

CAULIFLOWER POLONAISE

LEEKS AU GRATIN

STIR-FRY CABBAGE AND COURGETTES

RIBBON VEGETABLES

BRAISED MIXED VEGETABLES

RATATOUILLE

SWISS RÖSTI

SPANISH RICE

RISOTTO

POTATOES AU GRATIN

SWEET AND SOUR RED CABBAGE CASSEROLE

CHIP POTATOES

Herring salad

METAL BLADE

**625-g (1 lb 7-oz) jar pickled
  herrings
234 g (10 oz) pickled beetroot
25 g (1 oz) butter
30 ml (2 level tbsp) flour
salt and freshly ground pepper
pinch of sugar
1 medium eating apple
2 potatoes, cooked, skinned
  and diced**

1

Drain and dice the herrings,
reserving the pickling juice. Drain
and dice the beetroot, reserving
the pickling juice. Pour 175 ml
(6 fl oz) herring pickling juice and
50 ml (2 fl oz) beetroot pickling
juice in a saucepan and bring to a
boil; remove from the heat.

2

Fit the metal blade and place the
butter and flour in the bowl. Mix
until well blended then pour in the
hot liquid and mix, using a pulse
action, until smooth. Pour into the
saucepan and bring to a boil,
stirring. Add salt, pepper and sugar
and simmer for 2–3 minutes,
stirring. Remove from the heat,
cover with greaseproof paper and
cool completely.

3

When the sauce is cold, peel, core
and dice the apple. Fold the
herring, apple and potato into the
sauce. Cover and chill in the
refrigerator before serving.

Serves 4

Danish cucumber salad

SLICING DISC
METAL BLADE

**2 small cucumbers
5 ml (1 level tsp) salt**

For the dressing
**small bunch of fresh dill weed
100 ml (4 fl oz) white wine
  vinegar
50 g (2 oz) sugar
freshly ground pepper**

1

Fit the slicing disc. Wipe the
cucumbers and slice them very
thinly. Sprinkle with the salt and
leave to stand for 1 hour. Drain
well, rinse and pat dry with
absorbent kitchen paper.

2

Fit the metal blade and mix all the
ingredients for the dressing until
dill weed is finely chopped. Add
the dressing to the cucumbers and
stir together until well mixed.
Cover the salad and chill
thoroughly before serving.

Serves 4

Coleslaw

METAL BLADE
SLICING DISC
GRATING DISC

**small piece of onion, skinned
little fresh parsley (optional)
$\frac{1}{2}$ hard white cabbage, washed
  and cut in wedges
1 large carrot, peeled
about 75 ml (5 tbsp) salad
  cream or mayonnaise
5 ml (1 level tsp) sugar
salt and freshly ground pepper
few drops of lemon juice**

1

Fit the metal blade and chop the
onion finely. Add the parsley (if
used) and chop finely.

2

Fit the slicing disc and shred the
cabbage finely.

3

Fit the coarse grating disc and
grate the carrot.

4

Mix the salad cream or
mayonnaise with the sugar, salt
and pepper and add enough
lemon juice to sharpen the
flavour.

5

Tip the contents of the food
processor into a large bowl and
toss with the dressing until lightly
coated, adding a little more salad
cream or mayonnaise if necessary.

Serves 4

Waldorf salad

METAL BLADE
SLICING DISC

450 g (1 lb) eating apples
lemon juice
2.5 ml ($\frac{1}{2}$ level tsp) sugar
150 ml ($\frac{1}{4}$ pint) mayonnaise
50 g (2 oz) shelled walnuts
$\frac{1}{2}$ head of celery, trimmed
1 lettuce

1

Peel and core the apples, slice half of them and dip the slices in lemon juice. Fit the metal blade and chop the rest using a pulse action. Remove the chopped apples and toss with 30 ml (2 tbsp) lemon juice, the sugar and 15 ml (1 tbsp) mayonnaise; leave to stand for about 30 minutes.

2

With the metal blade, chop the walnuts. Change to the slicing disc and slice the celery.

3

Just before serving, add the walnuts, celery and remaining mayonnaise to the apples and toss together. Serve in a bowl lined with lettuce leaves.

Serves 4

Spinach timbale

METAL BLADE
GRATING DISC

1 medium onion, skinned and
**   quartered**
25 g (1 oz) butter or block
**   margarine**
900 g (2 lb) fresh spinach,
**   washed and trimmed**
150 ml ($\frac{1}{4}$ pint) milk
150 ml (5 fl oz) single cream
50 g (2 oz) fresh white bread,
**   crusts removed**
50 g (2 oz) Gruyère cheese
4 eggs
pinch of grated nutmeg
salt and freshly ground pepper

1

Grease a 1.5-litre (2$\frac{1}{2}$-pint) soufflé dish or ring mould and line the base with greaseproof paper.

2

Fit the metal blade and chop the onion finely. Melt the butter in a saucepan, stir in the onion and cook gently for about 5 minutes until soft. Stir in the spinach and cook for a further 5 minutes until soft, stirring occasionally. Stir in the milk and cream and heat gently. Turn the mixture into the food processor and chop roughly, using a pulse action. Turn into a bowl and set aside.

3

Cut the bread in chunks, put in the food processor and chop to fine crumbs. Change to the coarse grating disc and grate the cheese.

Add the breadcrumbs and grated cheese to the spinach.

4

Beat the eggs in the processor and stir into the spinach mixture with the breadcrumbs, cheese, nutmeg, salt and pepper.

5

Turn the mixture into the prepared dish, cover with foil and place the dish in a roasting tin half-filled with hot water. Bake in the oven at 180°C (350°F) mark 4 for 1 hour until firm to the touch. The timbale is cooked when a knife inserted in the centre comes out clean.

6

Remove the dish from the water and leave for 5 minutes. Loosen the timbale from the sides of the dish with a knife then turn it out on to a warmed flat serving dish. If you wish, serve with a cheese sauce (see page 95).

Serves 6

French beans with courgettes and bacon

METAL BLADE
SLICING DISC

250 g (9 oz) French beans, topped and tailed
4 rashers streaky bacon, rinded
1 small onion, skinned and quartered
2 medium courgettes, trimmed
50 g (2 oz) butter or block margarine
salt and freshly ground pepper

1

Cut the beans into 2.5-cm (1-inch) pieces. Cook in boiling salted water for 10 minutes; drain well.

2

Fry the bacon in its own fat until crisp. Drain well and crumble.

3

Fit the metal blade and chop the onion finely; remove and set aside. Fit the slicing disc and slice the courgettes.

4

Melt the fat and sauté the onion until soft but not coloured. Add the courgettes and fry them quickly, tossing them lightly, until just tender. Stir in the crumbled bacon, beans and seasoning and cook for a further minute to heat through the beans and bacon.

Serves 6

Cauliflower polonaise

METAL BLADE

1 cauliflower, trimmed and washed
salt
25 g (1 oz) slice fresh white bread, crusts removed
1 egg, hard-boiled and shelled
25 g (1 oz) butter
little fresh parsley
15 ml (1 tbsp) lemon juice

1

Cook the whole cauliflower, stem downwards, in boiling salted water for 10–15 minutes, until the stalk is tender but still crisp. Drain well.

2

Cut the bread in chunks. Fit the metal blade and chop it to fine crumbs; remove and set aside. Chop the parsley. Remove and set aside. Chop the egg roughly.

3

Melt the butter in a small saucepan and sauté the breadcrumbs until golden. Take off the heat.

4

Add the chopped egg, 15 ml (1 tbsp) parsley, the lemon juice and salt to taste. Stir together to mix.

5

Place the whole cauliflower in a heated serving dish and sprinkle with the breadcrumb mixture.

Serves 6

Cauliflower polonaise

Cauliflower, incredibly enough, is a member of the cabbage clan, and its 'flower' is quite literally what it says it is: a flower stalk that's become thickened into a storage organ. In nutritional terms, it's one of the richest vegetables in the cabbage family, containing important amounts of folic acid (a B vitamin), calcium and iron, as well as the more usual vegetable vitamins. Remember, though, that the longer you cook it, the less vitamins there will be: try to cook cauliflower in as little water as possible, at as high a temperature as possible for the shortest possible time, and *always* use a lid.

Leeks au gratin

GRATING DISC
METAL BLADE
SLICING DISC

100 g (4 oz) streaky bacon, rinded
100 g (4 oz) Cheddar cheese
25 g (1 oz) shelled walnuts
25 g (1 oz) fresh white bread, crusts removed
300 ml ($\frac{1}{2}$ pint) milk
25 g (1 oz) butter or block margarine
45 ml (3 level tbsp) flour
salt and freshly ground pepper
2.5 ml ($\frac{1}{2}$ level tsp) dry mustard
4 medium leeks, trimmed

1

Chop the bacon with a knife and fry in its own fat for about 10 minutes until crisp.

2

Fit the grating disc, grate the cheese and set aside in two batches. Fit the metal blade and chop the nuts roughly; remove and add to one of the batches of cheese. Cut the bread in chunks then chop to fine crumbs. Mix the crumbs with the cheese and nuts and set aside.

3

Bring the milk to a boil and remove from the heat. Fit the metal blade and place the butter and flour in the bowl. Mix until well blended then pour in the hot milk and mix, using a pulse action, until smooth. Pour into the saucepan and bring to the boil, stirring. Add salt, pepper and mustard and simmer for 5 minutes, stirring occasionally, until the sauce has thickened.

4

Meanwhile, fit the slicing disc and slice the leeks. Wash them and blanch in boiling salted water for 2–3 minutes. Drain well and spoon the leeks into a lightly greased ovenproof dish.

5

Add the reserved grated cheese to the sauce and pour the sauce over the leeks. Sprinkle the bacon and the cheese mixture on top of the dish and place under a hot grill until crisp and golden brown.

Serves 4

Stir-fried cabbage and courgettes

METAL BLADE
SLICING DISC

1 large garlic clove, skinned
2 courgettes
225 g (8 oz) white cabbage
45 ml (3 tbsp) vegetable oil
10 ml (2 level tsp) salt
5 ml (1 level tsp) sugar

1

Fit the metal blade and chop the garlic; remove and set aside. Fit the slicing disc. Slice the courgettes. Remove the core from the cabbage and shred the leaves.

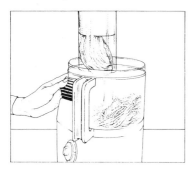

2

Heat the oil in a large flameproof casserole, add the garlic and cook until browned. Add the cabbage and courgettes to the oil and fry quickly, stirring until well coated.

3

Add the salt and sugar and stir-fry for 7–8 minutes more, until the vegetables are tender but crisp.

Serves 4

Ribbon vegetables

GRATING DISC

225 g (8 oz) courgettes, washed
225 g (8 oz) carrots, peeled
225 g (8 oz) parsnips or turnips, peeled
60 ml (4 tbsp) water
25 g (1 oz) butter or block margarine
5 ml (1 level tsp) sugar
5 ml (1 level tsp) salt

1

Fit the coarse grating disc and grate all the vegetables.

2

Tip them into a large saucepan, add the remaining ingredients and bring slowly to the boil. Cover and simmer gently for about 5 minutes or until the vegetables are tender but still crisp.

Serves 4

Braised mixed vegetables

CHIPPER DISC
SLICING DISC

225 g (8 oz) turnips, peeled
100 g (4 oz) mushrooms
225 g (8 oz) French beans, topped and tailed
40 g (1½ oz) butter or block margarine
225 g (8 oz) carrots, peeled
salt and freshly ground pepper
2.5 ml (½ level tsp) dried thyme

1

Fit the chipper disc and slice the turnips into chip shapes. Fit the slicing disc and slice the mushrooms. Cut the beans into 2.5-cm (1-inch) pieces and the carrots in half horizontally and then into julienne strips by hand.

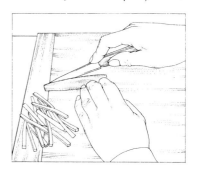

2

Melt the butter in a large saucepan and add the vegetables and remaining ingredients. Cover and cook for about 15 minutes, stirring occasionally, until the vegetables are just tender.

Serves 4–6

Ratatouille

SLICING DISC
METAL BLADE

1 large onion, skinned
30 ml (2 tbsp) olive oil
**1 garlic clove, skinned and
    crushed**
1 large aubergine
**1 green pepper, seeded and
    quartered**
**4 large tomatoes, skinned or
    398-g (14-oz) can tomatoes**
225 g (8 oz) courgettes
salt and freshly ground pepper
fresh parsley to garnish

1

Fit the slicing disc and slice the
onion. Heat the oil in a large
saucepan and add the onion and
crushed garlic. Fry for 5 minutes
until soft. Slice the aubergine in
half by hand.

2

With the slicing disc, slice the
aubergine and add to the pan. Fry
for 5 minutes. Slice the pepper and
add to the pan and cook for a
further 5 minutes. Slice the fresh
tomatoes and courgettes. Add the
fresh tomatoes or can of tomatoes
with their juice, the courgettes
and salt and pepper to the pan.

Cover and simmer gently for 45
minutes–1 hour until the
vegetables are tender, stirring
occasionally.

3

Meanwhile, with the metal blade,
chop the parsley. Spoon the
ratatouille into a warmed serving
dish and sprinkle with parsley.

Serves 4–6

Swiss rösti

GRATING DISC

**350 g (12 oz) medium to small
    old potatoes**
salt and freshly ground pepper
40 g (1½ oz) butter

1

Scrub the potatoes and parboil in
salted water for 7 minutes.
Remove the skins.

2

Fit the coarse grating disc and
grate the warm potatoes.

3

Heat the butter in a frying pan;
when bubbling, tip all the potatoes
into the pan. Using a palette knife,
shape the edges to form a neat
round which is not too thick. Fry
gently for 5–7 minutes until
golden brown, then carefully turn,
using a wide spatula, and brown
the second side. Serve hot, with a
parsley garnish.

Serves 2–3

Spanish rice

METAL BLADE

4 rashers streaky bacon, rinded
1 onion, skinned and quartered
1 green pepper, seeded and quartered
knob of butter
225 g (8 oz) long grain rice
600 ml (1 pint) canned tomato juice
salt and freshly ground pepper

1

Fit the metal blade and chop the bacon, taking care not to mince it too finely; remove and set aside. Put the onion and pepper in the food processor and chop roughly.

2

Fry the bacon lightly for 2–3 minutes in the butter, add the onion and pepper and fry for about 5 minutes, until soft.

3

Stir in the rice, tomato juice, salt and pepper, bring to the boil, cover with a lid, reduce the heat and simmer gently for 14–15 minutes. Stir lightly with a fork and serve. Good with chicken or ham.

Serves 4

Risotto

METAL BLADE

225 g (8 oz) streaky bacon, rinded
1 large onion, skinned and quartered
4 large tomatoes, skinned
275 g (10 oz) long grain rice
900 ml (1½ pints) chicken stock
salt and freshly ground pepper
fresh parsley to garnish

1

Fit the metal blade and roughly chop the bacon; remove and set aside. Roughly chop the onion; remove and set aside. Chop the skinned tomatoes.

2

Cook the bacon in a large frying pan until crisp and the fat begins to run. Remove from the pan and add the onion and rice and fry in the bacon fat until well coloured.

3

Stir the tomatoes into the rice and cook for 2 minutes. Add the stock and seasoning and bring to the boil. Turn into a casserole, cover and cook in the oven at 190°C (375°F) mark 5 for 40 minutes.

4

Stir in the bacon pieces and cook for a further 10 minutes. With the metal blade, chop the parsley and use as a garnish.

Serves 6

Risotto

Few people realise how greatly one kind of rice can differ from another: 400 different varieties are grown in India alone, and the world total is around 10,000 types. Italian *arborio* rice is the best to use for this recipe, and is worth seeking out. Do remember, though, that risotto is *not* like fried rice, and the end result will *not* be a mound of dry, fluffy grains: the grains should be firm and swollen, but in a true risotto they will be surrounded by a thick, unctuous sauce, and the texture should be sloppy rather than stiff, sticky or dry.

Potatoes au gratin

SLICING DISC
METAL BLADE
GRATING DISC

4–5 medium potatoes, peeled
7.5 ml (1½ level tsp) salt
25 g (1 oz) butter
25 g (1 oz) fresh white bread,
  crusts removed
100 g (4 oz) Cheddar cheese

1

Fit the slicing disc and thinly slice the potatoes. Sprinkle them with salt and toss together until well mixed. Arrange them in layers in a greased ovenproof dish. Melt the butter and pour it over the potatoes.

2

Cut the bread in chunks. Fit the metal blade and chop the bread to fine crumbs. Change to the fine grating disc and grate the cheese. Mix the cheese and breadcrumbs and sprinkle over the potatoes. Bake in the oven at 220°C (425°F) mark 7 for about 1 hour until golden brown and bubbling.

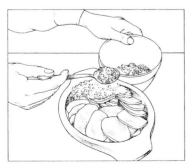

Serves 6

Sweet and sour red cabbage casserole

SLICING DISC

900 g (2 lb) red cabbage,
  trimmed and cut in wedges
2 onions, skinned
2 cooking apples, peeled and
  cored
10 ml (2 level tsp) sugar
salt and freshly ground pepper
bouquet garni
30 ml (2 tbsp) red wine vinegar
30 ml (2 tbsp) water
25 g (1 oz) butter or block
  margarine

1

Fit the slicing disc and shred the cabbage. Tip it into a colander and wash it thoroughly.

2

Slice the onions and apples.

3

Layer the cabbage, onion, apples, sugar and salt and pepper in a large casserole. Place the bouquet garni in the centre and spoon over the vinegar and water.

4

Cover and bake at 150°C (300°F) mark 2 for 2½ hours. Dot with butter before serving and stir well.

Serves 4

Chip potatoes

CHIPPING DISC

700–900 g (1½–2 lb) potatoes,
  peeled
oil or fat for deep frying
salt

1

Fit the chipping disc and slice the potatoes into chips. Tip them into a large bowl, cover with cold water and leave to soak for 30 minutes; pat dry.

2

Heat the oil to 190°C (375°F); a chip dropped into it should rise to the surface immediately, surrounded by bubbles.

3

Quarter-fill a frying basket with chips and lower into the oil. Cover and cook for 6–7 minutes. Drain on absorbent kitchen paper. Repeat with the remaining chips.

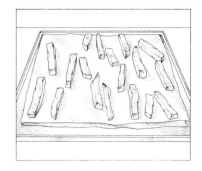

4

Reheat the oil and fry the chips for 3 minutes more until golden and crisp. Drain and sprinkle with salt.

Serves 4

SAUCES AND DRESSINGS

Savoury butters

METAL BLADE
PLASTIC BLADE

These butters can be used in many ways. Spread them on firm canapé bases to 'anchor' a topping, or pipe on to savouries for decoration. Alternatively form the butter into a roll, wrap it in cling film and chill; then slice the chilled butter into pats to serve with hot dishes such as grilled steak, chops, fish or chicken.

Anchovy butter

50-g (2-oz) can anchovy fillets, drained
100 g (4 oz) unsalted butter, softened

1

Fit the metal blade and mince the anchovies.

2

Add the butter. Starting on slow speed and increasing to maximum, or using a pulse action, mix well. Scrape down the sides of the bowl with a spatula and mix again until well creamed and thoroughly blended.

Green butter

50 g (2 oz) watercress
100 g (4 oz) butter, softened

1

Wash the watercress thoroughly and trim off the roots and any damaged leaves. Fit the metal blade and chop finely.

2

Add the butter. Starting on slow speed and increasing to maximum, or using a pulse action, mix well. Scrape down the sides of the bowl with a spatula and mix again until well creamed and thoroughly blended.

Blue cheese butter

50 g (2 oz) soft blue cheese
100 g (4 oz) unsalted butter, softened

1

Fit the metal blade. On slow speed, or using a pulse action, mix the blue cheese until softened.

2

Add the butter. Starting on slow speed and increasing to maximum, or using a pulse action, mix well. Scrape down the sides of the bowl with a spatula and mix again until well creamed and thoroughly blended.

Tomato butter

30 ml (2 level tbsp) tomato ketchup, or 10 ml (2 level tsp) tomato purée and 5 ml (1 level tsp) sugar
100 g (4 oz) butter, softened

1

Fit the plastic blade and put the tomato ketchup, or the tomato purée and sugar, with the butter in the bowl. Starting on slow speed and increasing to maximum, or using a pulse action, mix well. Scrape down the sides of the bowl with a spatula and mix again until well creamed and blended.

Lobster butter

50 g (2 oz) lobster coral
100 g (4 oz) butter, softened
freshly ground pepper

1

Fit the plastic blade and put the coral, butter and pepper in the bowl. Starting at slow speed and increasing to maximum, or using a pulse action, mix well. Scrape down the sides of the bowl with a spatula and mix again until well creamed and thoroughly blended.

Golden butter

yolks of 2 hard-boiled eggs
100 g (4 oz) butter, softened
freshly ground pepper

1

Fit the metal blade and chop the egg yolks finely.

2

Add the butter and pepper. Starting at slow speed and increasing to maximum, or using a pulse action, mix well. Scrape down the sides of the bowl with a spatula and mix again until well creamed and thoroughly blended.

Curry butter

100 g (4 oz) butter, softened
10 ml (2 level tsp) curry powder

1

Fit the plastic blade and put the butter and curry powder in the bowl. Starting on slow speed and increasing to maximum, or using a pulse action, mix well. Scrape down the sides of the bowl with a spatula and mix again until well creamed and thoroughly blended.

Ham butter

100 g (4 oz) cooked ham
100 g (4 oz) unsalted butter, softened

1

Fit the metal blade and mince the ham finely.

2

Add the butter. Starting on slow speed and increasing to maximum, or using a pulse action, mix well. Scrape down the sides of the bowl with a spatula and mix again until well creamed and thoroughly blended.

Sardine butter

4 canned sardines in oil, drained
100 g (4 oz) butter, softened

1

Fit the metal blade and mince the sardines finely.

2

Add the butter. Starting on slow speed and increasing to maximum, or using a pulse action, mix well. Scrape down the sides of the bowl with a spatula and mix again until well creamed and thoroughly blended.

Onion butter

½ small onion, skinned
100 g (4 oz) butter, softened

1

Fit the metal blade and chop the onion finely.

2

Add the butter. Starting on slow speed and increasing to maximum, or using a pulse action, mix well. Scrape down the bowl with a spatula and mix again until well creamed and blended.

Maître d'hôtel butter

small bunch of fresh parsley
100 g (4 oz) butter, softened
lemon juice
salt
cayenne pepper

1

Fit the metal blade and chop the parsley finely.

2

Add the butter, a squeeze of lemon juice and a little salt and cayenne pepper. Mix, starting on slow speed and increasing to maximum, or using a pulse action.

3

Scrape down the sides of the bowl with a spatula, adjust the seasoning and mix again until well creamed and thoroughly blended.

PESTO
PAGE 96

CHEESY HERB BAPS/WHOLEMEAL BREAD
PAGE 106

Pimiento butter

1 piece canned pimiento, drained
100 g (4 oz) butter, softened

1

Fit the metal blade and mince the pimiento finely.

2

Add the butter and mix, starting at slow speed and increasing to maximum or using a pulse action. Scrape down the sides of the bowl with a spatula and mix again until well creamed and blended.

Horseradish butter

100 g (4 oz) butter, softened
30 ml (2 level tbsp) creamed horseradish

1

Fit the plastic blade. Mix the butter and horseradish, starting on slow speed and increasing to maximum or using a pulse action. Scrape down the sides of the bowl with a spatula and mix again until well creamed and thoroughly blended.

White sauce

METAL BLADE

300 ml ($\frac{1}{2}$ pint) milk or milk and stock
15 g ($\frac{1}{2}$ oz) butter or block margarine
15 g ($\frac{1}{2}$ oz) flour
salt and freshly ground pepper

1

Pour the milk into a saucepan and bring to the boil. Remove from the heat and set aside.

2

Fit the metal blade and place the butter and flour in the bowl. Mix until blended then pour in the hot milk and mix, using a pulse action, until smooth.

3

Pour into the saucepan and bring to the boil, stirring. Season well and simmer for 5 minutes, stirring occasionally, until the sauce has thickened.

Makes 300 ml ($\frac{1}{2}$ pint)

Variations

Coating consistency white sauce
Prepare the sauce as above but use 25 g (1 oz) butter or block margarine and 25 g (1 oz) flour.

Cheese sauce Prepare the sauce as above, then remove from the heat and stir in 50 g–100 g (2–4 oz) mature Cheddar cheese, grated with the coarse grating disc, a pinch of dry mustard and a pinch of cayenne pepper, stirring until the cheese is melted.

Onion sauce With the metal blade, chop 2 onions. Simmer in salted water for 10–15 minutes until soft; drain well. Prepare a white sauce as above, replacing 150 ml ($\frac{1}{4}$ pint) milk with cooking liquid from the onions. Stir in the cooked onions and the grated rind of $\frac{1}{2}$ lemon when the sauce has thickened. Season to taste.
Makes 350 ml (12 fl oz)

Curry sauce Prepare the sauce as above, but stir in 60 ml (4 tbsp) finely chopped onion, 10 ml (2 level tsp) curry powder, 3.75 ml ($\frac{3}{4}$ level tsp) sugar and a pinch of ground ginger with the flour. Just before serving, stir in 5 ml (1 tsp) lemon juice.

Hot Thousand Island sauce
Prepare the sauce as above, but mix together 60 ml (4 tbsp) mayonnaise and 60 ml (4 tbsp) mild chilli sauce. Stir into the white sauce before serving.
Makes 350 ml (12 fl oz)

Caper sauce Prepare the sauce as above, but stir 15 ml (1 tbsp) capers and 5–10 ml (1–2 tsp) vinegar drained from the capers into the thickened white sauce. Season and reheat the sauce gently for 1–2 minutes before serving.

Hollandaise sauce

METAL BLADE OR WHISK

2 egg yolks
salt and freshly ground pepper
30 ml (2 tbsp) wine or tarragon vinegar
15 ml (1 tbsp) water
75–100 g (3–4 oz) butter

1

Fit the metal blade or whisk, put the egg yolks and seasoning in the bowl and mix well.

2

Put the vinegar and water in a small pan and boil until reduced to about 15 ml (1 tbsp). At the same time melt the butter in another pan and bring to the boil.

3

With the machine on slow speed add the boiling vinegar then butter in a slow, steady stream through the feeder tube. Increase to medium speed and mix well. Turn into a warmed serving dish. Serve with salmon and other fish dishes, asparagus or broccoli.

Serves 4

Note If the sauce is too sharp add a little more butter – it should be slightly piquant, almost thick enough to hold its shape. Serve warm rather than hot.

Tomato sauce

METAL BLADE

1 medium onion, skinned and quartered
25 g (1 oz) butter or block margarine
25 g (1 oz) plain flour
150 ml ($\frac{1}{4}$ pint) chicken stock
396-g (14-oz) can tomatoes
5 ml (1 level tsp) sugar
5 ml (1 level tsp) dried mixed herbs
15 ml (1 level tbsp) tomato purée
salt and freshly ground pepper
15 ml (1 tbsp) red wine (optional)

1

Fit the metal blade and chop the onion. In a saucepan fry the onion in the butter for about 10 minutes until soft.

2

Put the onion and butter in the food processor with the remaining ingredients and mix until smooth. Return to the saucepan, bring to the boil and cook for 3–4 minutes, stirring continuously.

Serves 4

Pesto

GRATING DISC
METAL BLADE

25 g (1 oz) Parmesan cheese
small bunch of fresh parsley
1 garlic clove, skinned
75 ml (5 tbsp) olive oil
30 ml (2 level tbsp) dried basil or 60 ml (4 level tbsp) fresh basil
1.25 ml ($\frac{1}{4}$ level tsp) grated nutmeg

1

Fit the grating disc and grate the Parmesan cheese. Change to the metal blade and chop the parsley and garlic finely.

2

Add the remaining ingredients and mix at medium speed until well blended. Toss with hot pasta.

Makes 125 ml (4 fl oz)

Pesto

This wonderful Ligurian sauce is increasingly available in jars here, but if you can make your own with fresh garden basil, a good virgin olive oil and freshly-grated Parmesan, then you'll find the difference stupendous. Look out for pine kernels in Italian delicatessens: if you manage to buy them, add 1oz at the same time as you combine the other ingredients. It will give a richer, stronger flavour to the resulting sauce.

Aïoli

METAL BLADE
WHISK

2 garlic cloves, skinned
2 egg yolks
salt and freshly ground pepper
300 ml ($\frac{1}{2}$ pint) olive oil
15 ml (1 tbsp) lemon juice

1

Fit the metal blade and chop the garlic very finely.

2

Change to the whisk and put the egg yolks and seasoning in the bowl; whisk briefly to mix. Switch to slow speed, or use a pulse action, and add the oil very gradually through the feeder tube, whisking continuously on slow speed until the sauce is smooth and thick. Add the lemon juice and whisk again to mix.

Makes 300 ml ($\frac{1}{2}$ pint)

Mayonnaise

WHISK OR METAL BLADE

1 egg yolk
2.5 ml ($\frac{1}{2}$ level tsp) dry mustard
salt and freshly ground pepper
1.25 ml ($\frac{1}{4}$ level tsp) sugar
about 150 ml ($\frac{1}{4}$ pint) vegetable oil
15 ml (1 tbsp) white wine vinegar

1

Fit the whisk or metal blade. Put the egg yolk in the bowl with the seasonings and sugar. Mix thoroughly on high speed then switch to slow, or use a pulse action, and add the oil gradually through the feeder tube, until the sauce is thick and smooth.

2

Add the vinegar gradually and mix thoroughly. If liked, lemon juice may be used instead of vinegar.

Makes 150 ml ($\frac{1}{4}$ pint)

Variations

Using 150 ml ($\frac{1}{4}$ pint) mayonnaise as a basis, add a flavouring as follows:

Caper Add 10 ml (2 tsp) chopped capers, 5 ml (1 tsp) chopped pimiento and 2.5 ml ($\frac{1}{2}$ tsp) tarragon vinegar. Goes well with fish.
Celery Add 15 ml (1 tbsp) chopped celery and 15 ml (1 tbsp) chopped chives.
Cream Add 60 ml (4 tbsp) whipped cream. Goes well with salads containing fruit, chicken or rice.
Cucumber Add 30 ml (2 tbsp) finely chopped cucumber and 2.5 ml ($\frac{1}{2}$ level tsp) salt. Goes well with fish salads, especially crab, lobster and salmon.
Herbs Add 30 ml (2 tbsp) chopped chives and 15 ml (1 tbsp) chopped parsley.
Horseradish Add 15 ml (1 tbsp) horseradish sauce.
Piquant Add 5 ml (1 tsp) tomato ketchup, 5 ml (1 tsp) chopped olives and a pinch of paprika.
Tomato Add $\frac{1}{2}$ tomato, skinned and diced, 1 spring onion, chopped, 1.25 ml ($\frac{1}{4}$ level tsp) salt and 5 ml (1 tsp) vinegar or lemon juice.
Blue cheese Add 25 g (1 oz) crumbled blue cheese.

Mayonnaise

There are nearly as many theories as to the origin of mayonnaise as there are varieties and flavourings for it. What seems certain is that it originated somewhere amongst the olive trees of the Mediterranean, probably south of the Pyrenees.

Modern electrical equipment has again made a difficult kitchen task into a rapid and easy one: remember to have all the ingredients at room temperature, though, and add the first few teaspoonsful of oil very gingerly. If the mayonnaise should fail to emulsify or it curdles, try adding a few drops of boiling water.

French dressing

WHISK OR METAL BLADE

90 ml (6 tbsp) vegetable oil
30 ml (2 tbsp) vinegar (see
below) or lemon juice
1.25 ml ($\frac{1}{4}$ level tsp) sugar
2.5 ml ($\frac{1}{2}$ level tsp) mustard, eg.
wholegrain, Dijon, French,
or mustard powder
salt and freshly ground pepper

1

Fit the whisk or metal blade. Place all the ingredients in the bowl and mix until well blended. The oil separates out on standing, so mix the dressing again if necessary immediately before use. The dressing can be stored in a bottle or screw-topped jar for up to a year in the refrigerator, but shake it up vigorously before serving.

Note The proportion of oil to vinegar can be varied according to taste. Wine, herb, cider or flavoured vinegars, or lemon juice, may be used, or use a mixture of half vinegar and half lemon juice.

Makes 120 ml (8 tbsp); if a recipe calls for 150 ml ($\frac{1}{4}$ pint) dressing, add an extra 15 ml (1 tbsp) oil and 15 ml (1 tbsp) vinegar

Variations

Fresh herb vinaigrette Add 15 ml (1 tbsp) chopped fresh parsley or 15 ml (1 tbsp) chopped fresh mint or 10 ml (2 tsp) snipped fresh chives, or a mixture of all three.
Mustard vinaigrette Add 15 ml (1 tbsp) wholegrain mustard.
Bombay dressing Add a large pinch of curry powder, 1 finely chopped hard-boiled egg and 10 ml (2 tsp) chopped onion.
Curry vinaigrette Add 5 ml (1 level tsp) curry powder.

French dressing

Salad dressings are often thrown together very casually with indifferent ingredients. This is a shame, for the taste of the dressing will determine at least half of the taste of the finished salad. Try to choose your oil for its flavour—olive, walnut or hazelnut oil if you like a strong flavour; sunflower or groundnut oil if you like a clean, neutral flavour—as well as your vinegar, which should be a wine or cider vinegar, *never* malt.

Remember the old adage, you need four people to make a good dressing: a spendthrift for the oil, a miser for the vinegar, a wise man for the salt, and a madman for the pepper. Imitate each in turn, and you won't go far wrong.

Mint sauce

METAL BLADE

small bunch of mint, washed
10 ml (2 level tsp) sugar
15 ml (1 tbsp) boiling water
15–30 ml (1–2 tbsp) vinegar

1

Fit the metal blade. Put the mint leaves only with the sugar in the bowl and chop finely.

2

Put in a sauceboat, add the boiling water and stir until the sugar is dissolved. Stir in vinegar to taste. The sauce should be left for 1 hour before serving. Serve with lamb.

Serves 4

Cranberry sauce

METAL BLADE

225 g (8 oz) sugar
300 ml ($\frac{1}{2}$ pint) water
225 g (8 oz) cranberries
15 ml (1 tbsp) port

1

Dissolve the sugar in the water and boil for 5 minutes. Add the cranberries and simmer for about 10 minutes or until the berries burst. Leave to cool a little.

2

Fit the metal blade and put the sauce in the bowl with the port. Chop to a smooth purée and leave to go cold. Serve with turkey.

Makes about 600 ml (1 pint)

Béarnaise sauce

METAL BLADE

few sprigs of fresh tarragon
1 shallot, skinned and
**   quartered**
60 ml (4 tbsp) wine or tarragon
**   vinegar**
75 g (3 oz) butter
2 egg yolks
salt and freshly ground pepper

1

Fit the metal blade and chop the tarragon. Add the shallot and chop finely. Put in a small saucepan with the vinegar over a gentle heat and reduce by boiling to about 15 ml (1 tbsp). At the same time, melt the butter in another pan and bring to the boil.

2

Put the egg yolks and seasoning in the food processor and mix well.

3

With the machine on slow speed or using a pulse action, add the boiling vinegar then butter in a slow, steady stream through the feeder tube. Increase to medium speed or still using a pulse action, mix well. Turn into a warm serving dish. Serve with steaks and grills.

Serves 4

Note   15 ml (1 tbsp) vinegar can be replaced by 15 ml (1 tbsp) water to give a slightly less piquant sauce which some people prefer.

Tartare sauce

WHISK
METAL BLADE

300 ml ($\frac{1}{2}$ pint) mayonnaise
**   (see page 97)**
2 sprigs of fresh tarragon or 12
**   chives**
4 sprigs of parsley
45 ml (3 tbsp) capers
4 small gherkins
15 ml (1 tbsp) lemon juice or
**   tarragon vinegar**

1

Fit the whisk or metal blade and make the mayonnaise. Transfer to a bowl.

2

Fit the metal blade and place the herbs, capers and gherkins in the bowl. Process until finely chopped. Add the mayonnaise and vinegar and process briefly until evenly mixed. Serve with fish.

Makes 300 ml ($\frac{1}{2}$ pint)

PRESERVES

Seville Orange Marmalade

Banana Chutney

Apple Ginger Jam

Mixed Sweet Chutney

Cherry Mincemeat

Seville orange marmalade

JUICE EXTRACTOR
SLICING DISC
METAL BLADE

1.5 kg (3 lb) Seville oranges, washed
juice of 2 lemons
3.6 litres (6 pints) water
3 kg (6 lb) sugar

1

Halve the oranges, fit the juice extractor and squeeze out the juice and pips. Tie the pips and any extra membrane that has come away during squeezing in a piece of muslin.

2

Cut the orange peels in half. Fit the slicing disc and slice the peel quarters. Transfer to a bowl.

3

Fit the metal blade and chop batches of the sliced peel, using a pulse action, to the thickness preferred.

4

Place the peel in a preserving pan with the fruit juices, water and muslin bag. Simmer gently for about 2 hours until the peel is really soft and the liquid reduced by about half.

5

Remove the muslin bag, squeezing it well and allowing the juice to run back into the pan.

6

Add the sugar, stirring until it has dissolved, then boil the mixture rapidly for about 15 minutes.

7

Test for a set (see page 102) and, when setting point is reached (105°C, 221°F), take the pan off the heat and remove any scum with a slotted spoon.

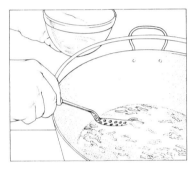

8

Ladle into warmed jars, cover with waxed paper discs and seal with cellophane and rubber bands.

Makes about 5 kg (10 lb)

Banana chutney

METAL BLADE
SLICING DISC

900 g (2 lb) cooking apples, peeled and cored
225 g (8 oz) onions, skinned and quartered
225 g (8 oz) stoned dates
1.8 kg (4 lb) bananas, peeled
10 ml (2 level tsp) salt
350 g (12 oz) demerara sugar
30 ml (2 level tbsp) ground ginger
1.25–2.5 ml ($\frac{1}{4}$–$\frac{1}{2}$ level tsp) cayenne pepper
600 ml (1 pint) malt vinegar

1

Cut the apples up roughly. Fit the metal blade and chop the apples. Put them in a preserving pan. Chop the onions and add to the apples. Chop the dates and add.

2

Fit the slicing disc and slice the bananas. Add to the pan with all the remaining ingredients.

3

Bring to the boil then simmer gently, uncovered, for about 1 hour until soft and pulpy. Stir occasionally during cooking.

4

Spoon into warm jars and cover with vinegar-proof covers. Store in a cool place.

Makes about 3.4 kg ($7\frac{1}{2}$ lb)

Apple ginger jam

SLICING DISC
METAL BLADE

1.8 kg (4 lb) cooking apples
900 ml (1½ pints) water
grated rind and juice of 3
**   lemons**
225 g (8 oz) preserved ginger
**   in syrup**
1.8 kg (4 lb) sugar

1

Peel and core the apples and tie
the peel and cores in muslin. Fit
the slicing disc; slice the apples.

2

Put the apples, the muslin bag,
water, lemon rind and juice in a
preserving pan. Bring to the boil
then simmer uncovered until the
apples are really soft and pulped.
Remove the muslin bag.

3

Fit the metal blade and chop the
ginger coarsely. Add to the apple
pulp with 45 ml (3 tbsp) of the
ginger syrup and the sugar.

4

Stir until the sugar has dissolved
then bring to the boil, stirring
constantly, and boil rapidly to
105°C (221°F). Test for a set.

5

Allow the jam to cool slightly then
spoon into warm jars and cover
with waxed paper discs and
cellophane jam pot covers.

Makes about 3.2 kg (7 lb)

Apple ginger jam

To test for a set: If you have no
thermometer, spoon a little
jam onto a cold saucer or a
plate and allow it to cool.
Then push your forefinger
across the top of the jam. If
the surface wrinkles, the jam
is ready.

Mixed sweet chutney

METAL BLADE

¾ medium cucumber, washed
450 g (1 lb) tomatoes, skinned,
**   halved and seeded**
700 g (1½ lb) marrow, peeled
**   and seeded**
1.1 litres (2 pints) malt vinegar
350 g (12 oz) demerara sugar
25 g (1 oz) salt
15 g (½ oz) ground turmeric
2.5 ml (½ level tsp) ground
**   mace**
2.5 ml (½ level tsp) ground
**   mixed spice**
15 g (½ oz) dried root ginger
2.5 ml (½ level tsp) celery seed

1

Fit the metal blade and chop the
cucumber finely; tip it into a
preserving pan. Chop the
tomatoes and add to the pan.
Chop the marrow finely and add
to the pan. Add the vinegar, sugar,
salt, ground spices and the ginger
and celery seed tied in muslin.

2

Stir, bring to the boil and simmer
uncovered for about 4 hours, until
dark in colour and of a fairly thick
consistency.

3

Remove the muslin bag of spices, spoon the chutney into warm jars and cover with vinegar-proof covers. Store in a cool place.

Makes about 900 g (2 lb)

Cherry mincemeat

METAL BLADE
GRATING DISC (OPTIONAL)

50 g (2 oz) shelled walnuts
50 g (2 oz) mixed candied peel
100 g (4 oz) currants, cleaned
100 g (4 oz) stoned raisins, cleaned
100 g (4 oz) sultanas, cleaned
50 g (2 oz) glacé cherries
100 g (4 oz) cooking apples, peeled and cored
100 g (4 oz) shredded suet
225 g (8 oz) demerara sugar
5 ml (1 level tsp) ground mixed spice
brandy or rum to mix

1

Fit the metal blade and chop the nuts; remove and set aside. Chop the candied peel and add it to the chopped nuts.

2

Add the currants, raisins, sultanas, cherries and apples, cut in chunks. Chop on high speed until finely minced, but do not overprocess. Turn the mixture into a large bowl with the nuts and peel.

3

Stir in the suet, sugar, spice and enough spirit to give a moist mixture. Stir well and leave to stand, covered, for 2 days.

4

Stir well again and spoon into jars. Cover with waxed paper discs and cellophane jam pot covers and allow to mature for at least 2 weeks before using.

Makes about 1 kg (2¼ lb)

Cherry mincemeat

In the old days, mincemeat was exactly that: ground, spiced, sweetened mutton or beef, sometimes mixed with dried fruit. You can still taste this combination in a small French town called Pézenas in the Midi: Clive of India took the recipe there when he rented a nearby chateau, and it's stayed on for the last 200 years, the mince pies being sold as *petits pâtés de Pézenas*. We, meanwhile, have forgotten the meat element, keeping only the suet as a reminder of this foodstuff's more robust past. Cherries add a special fruity element to contemporary mincemeat, and the addition of alcohol always gives mincemeat a great lift.

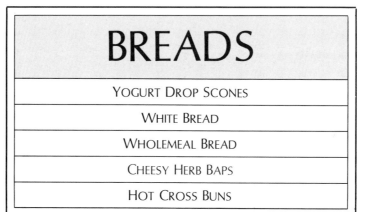

BREADS

Yogurt drop scones

PLASTIC BLADE

**142 ml (5 oz) natural yogurt
1 egg
50 g (2 oz) plain flour
pinch of salt
grated rind of 1 lemon
30 ml (2 tbsp) lemon juice
vegetable oil for frying
caster sugar**

1

Fit the plastic blade and put the first six ingredients in the bowl. Mix until smooth, starting on slow speed and increasing to maximum, or using a pulse action.

2

Heat a little oil in a large frying pan. Pour in 15 ml (1 tbsp) of batter at a time and cook for 1–2 minutes on each side until golden brown.

3

Remove from the pan and drain on absorbent kitchen paper. Serve warm, sprinkled with caster sugar or spread with lemon curd or jam.

Makes about 14

White bread

PLASTIC BLADE

**15 g ($\frac{1}{2}$ oz) fresh yeast or 7.5 ml (1$\frac{1}{2}$ level tsp) dried yeast and a pinch of sugar
300 ml ($\frac{1}{2}$ pint) tepid water
450 g (1 lb) strong plain white flour
5 ml (1 level tsp) salt
15 g ($\frac{1}{2}$ oz) lard**

1

If using dried yeast, sprinkle it into the water with the sugar and leave in a warm place for about 10 minutes until frothy. If using fresh yeast, crumble into the water. Fit the plastic blade and put the flour and salt into the bowl. Cut the lard into small pieces, add to the flour and mix, using a pulse action, until it resembles fine breadcrumbs.

2

Slowly pour in the yeast liquid through the feeder tube and mix until the dough forms a ball. Do not mix for more than 5–10 seconds after the ball forms.

3

Cover with a clean cloth and leave to rise in a warm place for about 1 hour until the dough is doubled in size and springs back when gently pressed with a floured finger.

4

Mix the dough briefly, using a pulse action, to knock out the air bubbles. Do not over-mix. Place in a greased 900-g (2-lb) loaf tin. Cover the tin with a clean cloth and leave to prove for about 1 hour until the dough comes to the top of the tin.

5

Bake in the oven at 230°C (450°F) mark 8 for 30–40 minutes until risen and golden brown. Turn out and cool on a wire rack.

Makes one 900-g (2-lb) loaf

White bread

There are few things more satisfying to make for oneself than bread, and the number of changes one can ring on a basic loaf are numerous. Seeds and nuts can be incorporated into the dough or sprinkled on top of the finished loaf. You can experiment with different flours—each will alter both flavour and texture—or use milk instead of water to mix the dough.

Try forming different shapes with your dough: plaits can be made by dividing the dough into three long rolls and plaiting them together, or a twist by doing the same thing with two. Divide the loaf into one two-third piece and one one-third piece to make a cottage loaf: put the smaller piece on top of the larger, and push your finger right through to the centre. Glaze with beaten egg before baking.

Wholemeal bread

PLASTIC BLADE

20 g ($\frac{3}{4}$ oz) fresh yeast or 7.5 ml ($1\frac{1}{2}$ level tsp) dried yeast and 5 ml (1 level tsp) sugar
365 ml ($12\frac{1}{2}$ fl oz) tepid water
450 g (1 lb) plain wholemeal flour
5 ml (1 level tsp) salt
15 g ($\frac{1}{2}$ oz) lard

1

If using dried yeast, sprinkle it into the water with the sugar and leave in a warm place for about 10 minutes until frothy. If using fresh yeast, crumble into the water. Fit the plastic blade and put the flour and salt into the bowl. Cut the lard into small pieces, add to the flour and mix, using a pulse action, until it resembles fine breadcrumbs.

2

Slowly pour in the yeast liquid through the feeder tube and mix until the dough forms a ball. Do not mix for more than 5–10 seconds after the ball forms.

3

Cover with a clean cloth and leave to rise in a warm place for about 1 hour until the dough is doubled in size and springs back when gently pressed with a floured finger.

4

Mix the dough briefly, using a pulse action, to knock out the air bubbles. Do not over-mix. Place in a greased 900-g (2-lb) loaf tin.

Cover the tin with a clean cloth and leave to prove for about 1 hour until the dough comes to the top of the tin.

5

Bake in the oven at 230°C (450°F) mark 8 for 15 minutes. Reduce the temperature to 200°C (400°F) mark 6 and bake for a further 30 minutes until risen and golden brown. Turn out and cool on a wire rack.

Makes one 900-g (2-lb) loaf

Cheesy herb baps

GRATING DISC
PLASTIC BLADE
METAL BLADE

50 g (2 oz) Cheddar cheese
25 g (1 oz) fresh yeast or 15 ml (1 tbsp) dried yeast
300 ml ($\frac{1}{2}$ pint) tepid milk
450 g (1 lb) strong plain white flour
10 ml (2 level tsp) salt
50 g (2 oz) butter or block margarine
15 ml (1 tbsp) chopped mixed fresh herbs

1

Fit the grating disc and grate the cheese, remove and set aside.

2

If using dried yeast, sprinkle into the milk and leave in a warm place for about 10 minutes until frothy. If using fresh yeast, crumble into the milk. Fit the plastic blade. Put 100 g (4 oz) flour and the yeast liquid in the bowl and mix on high speed to a smooth batter. Pour the batter into a bowl, cover with a clean cloth and leave in a warm place for 20 minutes until frothy.

3

Fit the metal blade and put the rest of the flour in the bowl with the salt; mix briefly. Cut the fat into small pieces and add to the flour. Mix until it resembles fine breadcrumbs.

4

Fit the plastic blade. Add the grated cheese and chopped herbs. With the machine running on slow speed or using a pulse action, add the yeast batter to the flour mixture through the feeder tube and mix to form a soft dough.

5

Cover the bowl with a clean cloth and leave to rise for about 1 hour until doubled in size.

6

Mix the dough briefly, using a pulse action, to knock out the air bubbles. Do not over-process. Lightly grease a baking sheet. Divide the dough into 8 portions and shape into rounds.

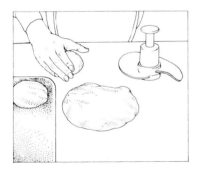

7

Place on the baking sheet, cover with a clean cloth and leave to prove in a warm place until doubled in size. Dust the tops lightly with flour.

8

Bake in the oven at 200°C (400°F) mark 6 for 15–20 minutes until risen and golden. Cool on a wire rack.

Makes 8

Hot cross buns

PLASTIC BLADE

25 g (1 oz) fresh yeast or 15 ml (1 tbsp) dried yeast
150 ml ($\frac{1}{4}$ pint) tepid milk
60 ml (4 tbsp) tepid water
450 g (1 lb) strong plain white flour
50 g (2 oz) butter, melted and cooled but not firm
1 egg, beaten
5 ml (1 level tsp) salt
2.5 ml ($\frac{1}{2}$ level tsp) ground cinnamon
2.5 ml ($\frac{1}{2}$ level tsp) ground nutmeg
50 g (2 oz) caster sugar
100 g (4 oz) currants
30–45 ml (2–3 tbsp) chopped mixed peel
shortcrust pastry made with 50 g (2 oz) plain flour (see page 119)

For the glaze
60 ml (4 tbsp) milk and water
45 ml (3 level tbsp) caster sugar

1

If using dried yeast, sprinkle into the milk and water and leave in a warm place for about 10 minutes until frothy. If using fresh yeast, crumble into the milk and water.

2

Fit the plastic blade. Put 100 g (4 oz) of the flour and the yeast liquid in the bowl and mix to a smooth batter. Set aside in a warm place for 20 minutes until frothy.

3

Add the melted butter and beaten egg to the frothy batter. Then add the remaining flour, the salt, spices, sugar, currants and chopped peel. Mix to a soft dough.

4

Cover the bowl with a clean cloth and leave in a warm place to rise until doubled in size.

5

Mix the dough briefly, using a pulse action, to knock out the air bubbles. Do not over-process. Shape the dough into 12 buns. Arrange on floured baking sheets, cover and leave to prove for 30 minutes until doubled in size.

6

Roll out the shortcrust pastry thinly; cut into 9-cm (3$\frac{1}{2}$-inch) strips. Damp them and lay two on each bun to make a cross. Bake in the oven at 190°C (375°F) mark 5 for 15–20 minutes until risen and golden brown.

7

Mix the milk, water and sugar and brush each hot bun twice with the glaze. Cool on a wire rack.

Makes 12

CAKES AND BISCUITS

SHORTBREAD
CHOCOLATE VIENNESE FINGERS
ALMOND CRISPS
BAKED FRUIT CHEESECAKE
UNCOOKED CHOCOLATE CAKE
MADEIRA CAKE
CARROT CAKE
LUXURY FRUIT CAKE
WALNUT COFFEE CAKE
BANANA TEA BREAD
SANDWICH CAKE
WHISKED SPONGE CAKE

Shortbread

METAL BLADE

150 g (5 oz) plain flour
25 g (1 oz) rice flour
50 g (2 oz) caster sugar
100 g (4 oz) butter or block
margarine, at room
temperature

1

Fit the metal blade and put the flours and sugar in the bowl. Mix briefly. Add the butter and mix on slow speed until the mixture resembles breadcrumbs. Switch to maximum speed and mix just until a dough forms.

2

Grease a baking sheet. Pack the dough into a rice-floured shortbread mould or an 18-cm (7-inch) sandwich tin. If using the mould, turn out on to the baking sheet and prick well.

3

Bake in the oven at 170°C (325°F) mark 3 until firm and golden – about 45 minutes. Turn out if necessary. When cool, dredge with sugar. Serve cut in wedges.

Makes 6–8

Note The rice flour is a traditional ingredient of shortbread, but it can be omitted, in which case use 175 g (6 oz) plain flour.

Chocolate Viennese fingers

PLASTIC BLADE

225 g (8 oz) plain flour
50 g (2 oz) icing sugar
30 ml (2 level tbsp) drinking
chocolate powder
2.5 ml ($\frac{1}{2}$ level tsp) baking
powder
225 g (8 oz) butter, softened, or
soft tub margarine
50 g (2 oz) plain chocolate,
melted
few drops vanilla flavouring

1

Sift together the flour, icing sugar, drinking chocolate and baking powder. Fit the plastic blade and put all the ingredients together in the bowl. Mix on maximum speed until smooth and creamy, stopping to scrape down the bowl once during mixing.

2

Using a piping bag fitted with a medium star nozzle, pipe the mixture into an equal number of finger shapes about 7.5 cm (3 inches) long on a greased baking sheet, keeping them spaced well apart.

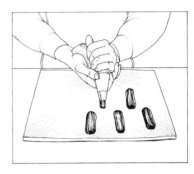

3

Bake in the oven at 170°C (325°F) mark 3 for about 15 minutes. Cool on a wire rack.

Makes about 18 fingers.

Variation

Omit the plain chocolate and drinking chocolate. Prepare the mixture as above and, using the same nozzle, pipe the mixture in two long continuous strips about 6.5 cm (2$\frac{1}{2}$ inches) wide, using a backward and forward zigzag movement. Bake as above. Whilst warm, mark across into 24 portions; break when cold.

Almond crisps

METAL BLADE
PLASTIC BLADE

75 g (3 oz) blanched almonds
125 g (4 oz) butter, softened
75 g (3 oz) caster sugar
1 egg yolk
few drops of almond
**   flavouring**
150 g (5 oz) self raising flour
egg white to glaze

1

Fit the metal blade and chop the almonds. Remove and set aside.

2

Fit the plastic blade and cream the butter and sugar together on maximum speed until pale and fluffy. Add the egg yolk and almond flavouring and mix again. Add the flour and mix until a smooth dough is formed.

3

Form the dough into about 24 even-sized balls. Place well apart on greased baking sheets and flatten slightly with the palm of your hand. Brush with egg white and place a little of the chopped almonds on top of each.

4

Bake in the oven at 190°C (375°F) mark 5 for 15 minutes until golden. Cool on baking sheets for 2–3 minutes, transfer to a wire rack.

Makes about 24

Baked fruit cheesecake

METAL BLADE
PLASTIC BLADE
WHISK

175 g (6 oz) self raising flour
50 g (2 oz) cornflour
175 g (6 oz) butter or block
**   margarine**
50 g (2 oz) icing sugar
good grating of nutmeg
3 eggs, separated
225 g (8 oz) full fat soft cheese
50 g (2 oz) caster sugar
grated rind of 1 lemon
142 ml (5 fl oz) soured cream
25 g (1 oz) chopped mixed peel
50 g (2 oz) seedless raisins
extra icing sugar for dusting

1

Grease and line a 20.5-cm (8-inch) square cake tin about 3.5 cm (2$\frac{1}{2}$ inches) deep.

2

Fit the metal blade, place the flours together in the bowl and add the butter cut in small pieces. Using a pulse action, mix until the mixture resembles breadcrumbs. Sift in the icing sugar and nutmeg and mix again briefly.

3

Add 1 egg yolk and mix until a stiff dough forms. Roll out half the mixture on to greaseproof paper, to measure 20.5 cm (8 inch) square. Lift into the prepared tin. Press lightly into the corners. Chill in the refrigerator for 15 minutes.

4

Bake in the oven at 180°C (350°F) mark 4 for 15 minutes. Allow to cool in the tin for 15 minutes.

5

Meanwhile, roll out the remaining pastry in the same way. Chill until ready to use.

6

Fit the plastic blade and mix together the cheese, caster sugar, and lemon rind until soft and creamy. Add 2 egg yolks, the soured cream and nutmeg and mix again until well blended. Turn into a large bowl and set aside.

7

Fit the whisk, whisk the egg whites until stiff and fold them into the cheese mixture with a large metal spoon. Fold in the chopped peel and raisins. Pour the mixture over the pastry base. Place the chilled pastry on top of the filling but do not press down. Remove the greaseproof paper.

8

Bake in the oven at 180°C (350°F) mark 4 for 40–45 minutes until firm. Cool in the tin then turn it out, cut into 9 squares and dust with icing sugar.

Serves 9

WALNUT COFFEE CAKE
PAGE 115

BROWN BREAD ICE CREAM
PAGE 121

Uncooked chocolate cake

METAL BLADE
PLASTIC BLADE

100 g (4 oz) plain sweet biscuits, petit beurre type
50 g (2 oz) digestive biscuits
50 g (2 oz) shelled walnuts
100 g (4 oz) butter or soft tub margarine
30 ml (2 level tbsp) caster sugar
75 g (3 oz) golden syrup
50 g (2 oz) cocoa powder
50 g (2 oz) plain chocolate
65 g (2½ oz) icing sugar

1

Fit the metal blade. Break the biscuits roughly into the bowl then chop to crumbs; remove and set aside. Chop the walnuts and add to the biscuit crumbs.

2

Fit the plastic blade and mix together 90 g (3½ oz) butter, the sugar and syrup until smooth and creamy. Add the biscuit crumbs, nuts and cocoa powder and mix until a dough forms.

3

Press the dough evenly into a 18-cm (7-inch) flan ring placed on a flat serving plate or board. Refrigerate overnight.

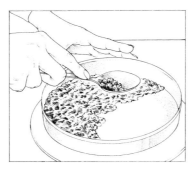

4

To make the icing put the chocolate, 15 ml (1 tbsp) water, the icing sugar and remaining butter in a small saucepan. Place over a very low heat until the chocolate has melted; stir until it reaches a coating consistency.

5

Remove the flan ring from the cake and spread the icing over the top. Leave to set.

Serves 8

Madeira cake

PLASTIC BLADE

175 g (6 oz) butter, softened, or soft tub margarine
175 g (6 oz) caster sugar
3 eggs, beaten
5 ml (1 tsp) vanilla flavouring
110 g (4 oz) plain flour
110 g (4 oz) self raising flour
15 ml (1 tbsp) milk
2–3 thin slices citron peel

1

Grease and line with greased greaseproof paper an 18-cm (7-inch) round cake tin.

2

Fit the plastic blade and cream the butter and sugar together on maximum speed until pale and fluffy. Keep scraping down the sides of the bowl to incorporate all of the butter.

3

Add the eggs and vanilla flavouring and mix again. Add the flour and milk and mix until just blended in.

4

Put the mixture into the tin and bake in the oven at 180°C (350°F) mark 4. After 20 minutes, put the citron peel across the cake and continue to cook for a further 50 minutes. Cool on a wire rack.

Serves 6–8

Carrot cake

GRATING DISC
METAL BLADE
PLASTIC BLADE

225 g (8 oz) carrots, peeled
100 g (4 oz) blanched almonds
225 g (8 oz) butter, softened, or
  soft tub margarine
225 g (8 oz) caster sugar
4 eggs
grated rind and juice of 1
  lemon
15 ml (1 tbsp) Kirsch (optional)
225 g (8 oz) self raising flour
225 g (8 oz) icing sugar
75 g (3 oz) marzipan
orange food colouring
angelica

1

Grease and line with greased
greaseproof paper a 20.5-cm
(8-inch) round cake tin.

2

Fit the coarse grating disc and
grate the carrots; remove and set
aside. Fit the metal blade and
chop the almonds coarsely;
remove and set aside.

3

Fit the plastic blade and cream the
butter and sugar together on
maximum speed until pale and
fluffy. Add the eggs, lemon rind
and juice, reserving 10 ml (2 tsp),
and kirsch if used and mix again.
Scrape down the bowl, add the
flour, carrots and almonds and mix
until just blended in.

4

Spoon the mixture into the cake
tin. Bake in the oven at 180°C
(350°F) mark 4 for 1½ hours until
well risen and golden brown. After
1 hour cover with foil to prevent
over-browning. The cake is
cooked when a skewer inserted in
the centre comes out clean. Cool
on a wire rack.

5

Preferably keep the cake until the
following day before icing and
serving. Sift the icing sugar into a
bowl and add the reserved lemon
juice and about 15 ml (1 tbsp)
warm water. The icing should be
thick enough to coat the back of a
spoon. Spread the icing on top of
the cake.

6

Fit the plastic blade and put the
marzipan and orange food
colouring in the bowl. Mix until the
colour is evenly blended then
shape it into small carrots; use
angelica for carrot tops. Decorate
the cake with the carrots.

Serves 8

Luxury fruit cake

METAL BLADE
PLASTIC BLADE

175 g (6 oz) currants
225 g (8 oz) sultanas
225 g (8 oz) seedless raisins
50 g (2 oz) chopped mixed peel
grated rind and juice of 2
  oranges
150 ml (¼ pint) sherry or
  brandy
50 g (2 oz) shelled walnuts
250 g (9 oz) plain flour
25 g (1 oz) self raising flour
225 g (8 oz) butter, softened, or
  soft tub margarine
225 g (8 oz) dark soft brown
  sugar
4 eggs, size 2
75 g (3 oz) glacé cherries

1

Combine the dried fruits and
mixed peel in a large basin. Stir in
the orange rind and juice and the
sherry or brandy. Press down well,
cover the basin and leave
to soak overnight.

2

Grease a 20.5-cm (8-inch) round
cake tin and line it with greased

greaseproof paper. Tie a double band of brown paper round the outside of the tin.

3

Fit the metal blade and chop the walnuts; remove and set aside.

4

Fit the plastic blade. Place the flours, butter, sugar and eggs in the bowl and mix on maximum speed until light and fluffy.

5

Scrape the mixture into the basin with the soaked fruits, add the cherries and chopped nuts and stir to mix evenly.

6

Turn the mixture into the prepared tin. Level the surface and make a slight hollow in the centre. Stand the tin on a layer of newspaper or brown paper. Bake in the oven at 150°C (300°F) mark 2 for about 3–$3\frac{1}{2}$ hours, the cake is cooked when a skewer inserted in the centre comes out clean. If over-browning after $2\frac{1}{2}$ hours cover with a thick layer of greaseproof paper. Leave in the tin until completely cold, then turn out. To store, wrap the cake in greaseproof paper, overwrap with foil or put in an airtight tin.

Serves 6–8

Walnut coffee cake

PLASTIC BLADE
METAL BLADE

50 g (2 oz) shelled walnuts
100 g (4 oz) butter, softened, or
**   soft tub margarine**
100 g (4 oz) caster sugar
2 eggs, size 2
15 ml (1 tbsp) coffee essence
100 g (4 oz) self raising flour
5 ml (1 level tsp) baking
**   powder**
coffee beans to decorate

For the coffee filling
225 g (8 oz) icing sugar
75 g (3 oz) butter or soft tub
**   margarine**
30 ml (2 tbsp) milk
20 ml (4 tsp) coffee essence

1

Grease two 18-cm (7-inch) sandwich tins and line the base of each with a round of greased greaseproof paper. Fit the metal blade and chop the walnuts.

2

Change to the plastic blade and cream the butter and sugar together on maximum speed until pale and fluffy. Add the eggs and coffee essence and mix again. Sift the flour and baking powder together into the bowl and mix until just blended in.

3

Turn the mixture into the prepared tins and level the surface.

4

Bake in the oven at 170°C (325°F) mark 3 for 20–30 minutes. Turn the cakes out and leave to cool on a wire rack.

5

To make the filling fit the plastic blade. Place the icing sugar in the bowl, add the butter or margarine, milk and coffee essence and mix until well creamed.

6

Sandwich the cakes together with some of the filling. Use the remainder to cover the top, and decorate with coffee beans.

Serves 6–8

Banana tea bread

METAL BLADE
PLASTIC BLADE

100 g (4 oz) shelled walnuts
450 g (1 lb) bananas, peeled
75 g (3 oz) butter, softened, or
**   soft tub margarine**
175 g (6 oz) sugar
2 eggs
200 g (7 oz) self raising flour
1.25 ml ($\frac{1}{4}$ level tsp)
**   bicarbonate of soda**
2.5 ml ($\frac{1}{2}$ level tsp) salt

1

Grease a loaf tin measuring 21.5 × 11.5 cm (6$\frac{1}{2}$ × 4$\frac{1}{2}$ inch) across the top and line the base with greased greaseproof paper.

2

Fit the metal blade and chop the nuts; remove and set aside. Put the bananas in the bowl and chop to a purée; remove and set aside.

3

Fit the plastic blade and cream the butter and sugar together on maximum speed until pale and fluffy. Add the eggs and mix again. Add the banana purée and mix on slow speed until well blended in.

4

Sift together the flour, bicarbonate of soda and the salt, add to the bowl and mix just until the flour is blended in. Do not over-mix. Add the nuts and mix briefly, using a pulse action.

5

Pour the mixture into the tin and bake in the oven at 180°C (350°F) mark 4 for about 1$\frac{1}{4}$ hours, until well risen and just firm. Turn out and cool on a wire rack. Keep for 24 hours before serving sliced and spread with butter.

Serves 6–8

Sandwich cake

PLASTIC BLADE

100 g (4 oz) butter, softened, or
**   soft tub margarine**
100 g (4 oz) caster sugar
2 eggs, size 2
100 g (4 oz) self raising flour
5 ml (1 level tsp) baking
**   powder**
jam or lemon curd to fill

1

Grease two 18-cm (7-inch) sandwich tins and line each base with a round of greased greaseproof paper.

2

Fit the plastic blade and cream the butter and sugar together on maximum speed until pale and fluffy. Add the eggs and mix again. Sift the flour and baking powder together into the bowl and mix until just blended in.

3

Divide the mixture evenly between the tins and spread it out smoothly. Bake in the oven at 170°C (325°F) mark 3 for 20–25 minutes.

4

Turn out to cool on a wire rack. When cold, sandwich the cakes together with jam or lemon curd.

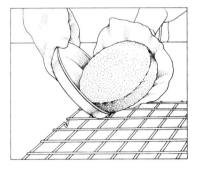

Serves 6–8

Sandwich cake

The British tea-time tradition, under something of a shadow at the moment as we all struggle to retain our figures, is in fact one of our greatest national culinary achievements, and it would be a tragedy if we were ever to lose our cake-baking skills. This sandwich cake is one of the simplest to make, yet it can be constantly varied: substitute 3 tablespoons of cocoa for 3 of flour for a chocolate sandwich, or stir in a little very strong coffee or grated orange or lemon peel for a coffee, orange or lemon sandwich. Flavour the butter icing of your choice using the same ingredients.

Whisked sponge cake

WHISK

3 eggs, size 2
100 g (4 oz) caster sugar
75 g (3 oz) plain flour
icing sugar (optional)
150 ml (5 fl oz) double or
** whipping cream**

1

Grease two 18-cm (7-inch) sandwich tins and dust them with a mixture of flour and caster sugar. Shake out any excess.

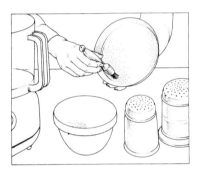

2

Fit the whisk and put the eggs and caster sugar in the bowl. Whisk at maximum speed until the mixture is pale and thick and has at least doubled in volume.

3

Switch to slow speed and add the flour a spoonful at a time through the feeder tube. Mix only for a few seconds until the flour is just blended in.

4

Divide the mixture between the tins and bake in the oven at 190°C (375°F) mark 5 for 20 minutes until well risen and the tops spring back when lightly touched. Turn out on to a wire rack to cool.

5

Fit the whisk again and whip the cream. Sandwich the cold cakes with cream and dust the top with icing sugar if you wish.

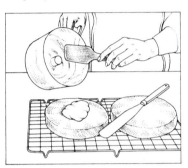

Serves 6–8

PASTRIES AND DESSERTS

SHORTCRUST PASTRY

PÂTE BRISÉE

FLAN PASTRY

RHUBARB FOOL

PEAR ICE CREAM

BROWN BREAD ICE CREAM

PEACH AND YOGURT ICE

CRÊPES SUZETTE

CHOCOLATE MOUSSE

BLACKBERRY AND APPLE AUTUMN PUDDING

APPLE BERRY FRUIT FOOL

PROFITEROLES

SYRUP TART

PINEAPPLE UPSIDE-DOWN PUDDING

Shortcrust pastry

METAL BLADE

225 g (8 oz) plain flour
pinch of salt
125 g (4 oz) fat, half lard and
half block margarine or
butter
about 40 ml (8 tsp) cold water

1

Fit the metal blade. Put the flour
and salt in the bowl. Cut the fat
into small pieces and add to the
flour. Mix on high speed, using a
pulse action, until the mixture
resembles fine breadcrumbs.

2

Sprinkle the water on the flour,
and mix, using a pulse action, until
a dough begins to form.

3

Mix briefly until the dough forms a
ball and leaves the side of the
bowl. Wrap loosely in greaseproof
paper and leave it to rest in the
refrigerate for up to 2 days.

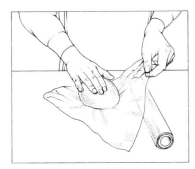

4

Roll the dough out on a lightly-
floured surface with a lightly-
floured rolling pin and shape as
required. Bake in the oven at 200–
220°C (400–425°F) mark 6–7 or as
the recipe directs.

To adjust this recipe for various
sizes of flan ring or tin allow:
100 g (4 oz) flour for a 15-cm
(6-inch) ring
150 g (5 oz) flour for an 18-cm
(7-inch) ring
200 g (7 oz) flour for a 20.5-cm
(8-inch) ring
250 g (9 oz) flour for a 23-cm
(9-inch) ring
Adjust other ingredients in
proportion. These amounts also
apply to Flan pastry and Pâte
brisée.

Pâte brisée

METAL BLADE

175 g (6 oz) plain flour
pinch of salt
pinch of icing sugar
125 g (4 oz) butter

1

Fit the metal blade. Put the flour,
salt and icing sugar in the bowl
and mix briefly.

2

Cut the butter in small pieces and
add to the flour. Mix on high
speed until the mixture resembles
fine breadcrumbs.

3

Switch to slow speed and add a
little chilled water through the
feeder tube, mixing just enough to
form a dough.

4

Gather the dough together with
one hand, wrap it in cling film or
foil and leave in the refrigerator to
rest for about 30 minutes.

5

Leave the dough at room
temperature for a little while
before rolling out, so that it
becomes malleable again. If it is
hard at first, hit it with a rolling pin,
but do not knead again.

Note This is a rich shortcrust
pastry suitable for quiches and
tarts. It is light and crisp but
because the ratio of fat to flour is
very high, is rather fragile.

Flan pastry

METAL BLADE

100 g (4 oz) plain flour
pinch of salt
5 ml (1 level tsp) caster sugar
75 g (3 oz) butter or block
**   margarine and lard**
1 egg, beaten

1

Fit the metal blade. Put the flour, sugar and salt in the bowl and mix together briefly.

2

Cut the fat in small pieces and add to the flour. Mix on high speed until the mixture resembles fine breadcrumbs.

3

Switch to slow speed and add the egg gradually through the feeder tube, mixing just until a dough forms. Wrap in cling film or foil and leave in the refrigerator to rest for about 30 minutes.

4

Roll out as for shortcrust pastry and use as required. Bake in the oven at 200°C (400°F) mark 6.

Rhubarb fool

SLICING DISC
METAL BLADE
WHISK

450 g (1 lb) rhubarb, trimmed
30 ml (2 tbsp) golden syrup
30 ml (2 tbsp) dark rum
**   (optional)**
300 ml (10 fl oz) double cream

1

Fit the slicing disc and slice the rhubarb. Put in a heavy pan with the golden syrup, 60 ml (4 tbsp) water and the rum, if used. Simmer, covered, over a low heat for 10 minutes or until the rhubarb is tender. Leave to cool.

2

Fit the metal blade, add the rhubarb and chop to a purée. Transfer to a bowl. Fit the whisk and whip the cream. Place half in a piping bag fitted with a star nozzle and set aside. Add the rhubarb purée to the remaining cream in the bowl and whisk again until the rhubarb is well mixed. Spoon into individual glasses and chill well. Decorate with the reserved cream.

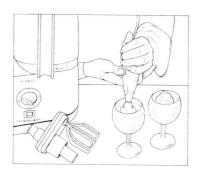

Serves 6–8

Pear ice cream

METAL BLADE
WHISK

700 g (1½ lb) ripe pears
450 ml (¾ pint) milk
4 egg yolks
100 g (4 oz) sugar
juice of 1 lemon
300 ml (10 fl oz) whipping
**   cream**

1

Peel, quarter and core the pears. Bring the milk to a boil, reduce the heat, add the pears and poach gently for 5–10 minutes until the fruit is quite tender.

2

Fit the metal blade, add the egg yolks and sugar and mix until smooth. Strain the hot milk on to the mixture and mix well. Return the custard to the saucepan and cook it gently over a low heat, stirring all the time, until it coats the back of a wooden spoon. Do not boil. Leave to cool slightly.

3

While still warm, place the poached pears in the bowl and mix to a purée. Add the custard and lemon juice and mix well. Pour into a shallow freezer container and leave to cool. Freeze for 2 hours until mushy.

4

Fit the whisk. Place the cream in the bowl and whisk until it holds its shape then transfer to a bowl.

5

Fit the metal blade, and mix the pear mixture until smooth. Fold into the whipped cream and freeze again for at least 6 hours until the ice cream becomes firm. Place in the refrigerator for about 30 minutes before serving.

Serves 8

Pear ice cream

We in Britain eat fewer pears per person than any of our fellow EEC citizens: a paltry 3 lb a year on average. One reason for this may be the near-stranglehold exerted on the market by Conference pears, which often make dull eating: other, wonderful, dessert pears such as Comice, Williams and Beurre d'Amanlis are harder and harder to come by. If Conference pears are less exciting for dessert than they might be, they are at least good to cook with, retaining texture and flavour better than many other varieties. They're an excellent choice for this rich yet delicately-flavoured ice cream.

Brown bread ice cream

WHISK
METAL BLADE

300 ml (10 fl oz) double cream
150 ml (5 fl oz) single cream
2.5 ml ($\frac{1}{2}$ tsp) vanilla flavouring
grated rind of 1 lemon
50 g (2 oz) icing sugar, sifted
100 g (4 oz) fresh brown bread, crusts removed
50 g (2 oz) soft brown sugar

1

Fit the whisk and whisk together the creams until stiff. Fold in the vanilla flavouring, lemon rind and icing sugar. Spoon the mixture into a shallow plastic container and freeze for 1 hour or until the cream is starting to freeze round the edges.

2

Meanwhile cut the bread in chunks. Fit the metal blade and chop the bread to fine crumbs. Spread the breadcrumbs out on a lightly oiled baking sheet and sprinkle over the brown sugar.

3

Bake in the oven at 200°C (400°F) mark 6 for 10–15 minutes, stirring occasionally, until the sugar caramelises and the crumbs are golden brown. Leave to cool.

4

Put the caramelised crumbs back in the food processor and chop briefly to break up any lumps; remove and set aside. Spoon the ice cream into the bowl and mix until smooth. Add the breadcrumbs and mix again until evenly blended. Spoon the mixture back into the container and freeze until firm.

5

Transfer to the refrigerator for 30 minutes to soften before serving.

Serves 6

Peach and yogurt ice

METAL BLADE
PLASTIC BLADE
WHISK

3 large peaches
175 g (6 oz) sugar
150 ml ($\frac{1}{4}$ pint) water
juice of $\frac{1}{2}$ lemon
2 eggs, separated
300 ml (10 fl oz) natural yogurt

1

Put the peaches in a large bowl, cover with boiling water and leave for 1 minute. Drain and skin the peaches, halve them and discard the stones. Fit the metal blade and chop the peaches to a purée; remove and set aside.

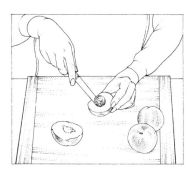

2

Put the sugar in a saucepan with the water and stir over gentle heat until the sugar is dissolved. Bring to the boil and boil for 5 minutes.

3

Fit the plastic blade, put the egg yolks in the bowl and mix until pale and frothy. Switch to slow speed and pour the hot syrup

slowly in through the feeder tube. Add the peach purée, mix well and leave to cool. Then add the yogurt and mix in thoroughly.

4

Pour the mixture into a shallow plastic container and freeze for about 1 hour.

5

Fit the whisk and pour the egg whites into the bowl. Whisk the egg whites until stiff; remove and set aside.

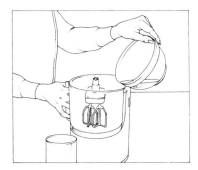

6

Fit the metal blade, spoon in the peach mixture and beat on high speed until smooth. Spoon in the egg whites and mix in on slow speed or using a pulse action.

7

Return the mixture to the container and freeze again for 3–4 hours until firm. Transfer to the refrigerator for 30 minutes before serving.

Serves 6

Crêpes Suzette

PLASTIC OR METAL BLADE

50 g (2 oz) sugar
50 g (2 oz) butter
juice of 2 oranges
grated rind of 1 lemon
45 ml (3 tbsp) orange-flavoured liqueur
30 ml (2 tbsp) brandy

For the crêpes
125 g (4 oz) plain flour
pinch of salt
grated rind of $\frac{1}{2}$ orange
1 egg
15 g ($\frac{1}{2}$ oz) butter, melted
300 ml ($\frac{1}{2}$ pint) milk
butter for frying

1

Fit the plastic or metal blade. Put the flour, salt and orange rind in the bowl and mix briefly. Add the egg, the melted butter and half the milk and mix until smooth, starting on slow speed and increasing to maximum or using a pulse action. Add the remaining milk through the feeder tube and mix again until thoroughly blended.

2

Heat a little butter in a 15–18 cm (6–7 inch) thick-based frying pan, pour off the excess and cook the pancakes in the usual way; keep them flat between two plates in a warm place.

3

Clean the pan, put in the sugar and heat gently, shaking the pan occasionally until the sugar has melted and turned golden brown. Remove the pan from the heat and add the butter, orange juice and lemon rind. Fold each pancake in half and then in half again to form a quarter-circle. Add the liqueur to the fruit juice, replace all the crêpes in the pan and simmer for a few minutes until reheated, spooning the sauce over them.

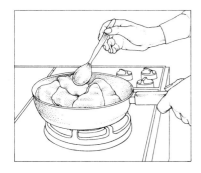

4

Warm the brandy, pour it over the crêpes, ignite it and serve at once.

Serves 4

Chocolate mousse

PLASTIC OR METAL BLADE
WHISK

450 g (1 lb) plain chocolate
25 g (1 oz) butter
8 eggs, separated
30 ml (2 tbsp) orange juice
300 ml (10 fl oz) whipping
    cream
chocolate curls to decorate

1

Break up the chocolate and put in a basin with the butter over a pan of hot water until melted. Remove from the heat.

2

Fit the plastic or metal blade and put the egg yolks in the bowl with the orange juice. Mix on high speed until well blended.

3

Add the melted chocolate to the bowl then switch to slow speed until mixed. Scrape the mixture into a bowl and set aside.

4

Fit the whisk and whisk the egg whites until stiff. Fold into the chocolate mixture with a large metal spoon.

5

Spoon into 8 small dishes and chill in the refrigerator until set. Whip the cream until set. Pipe on top of the mousses and decorate before serving.

Serves 8

Blackberry and apple autumn pudding

SLICING DISC

700 g (1½ lb) cooking apples, peeled, quartered and cored
225 g (8 oz) blackberries
45 ml (3 level tbsp) redcurrant jelly
50 g (2 oz) granulated sugar
22.5 ml (1½ tbsp) lemon juice
65 ml (2½ fl oz) water
8 trifle sponges
pouring cream to serve

1

Fit the slicing disc and thinly slice the apples. Put them in a large pan, add the blackberries, redcurrant jelly, sugar, lemon juice and water. Bring to the boil, cover and simmer until mushy.

2

Split the sponges in half lengthways. Use eight pieces to line the bottom and sides of a 900-ml (1½-pint) pudding basin.

3

Spoon the fruit mixture into the basin and top with the remaining sponge cakes. Stand the basin on a plate to catch any juice that spills. Place a small plate or saucer on top of the pudding with a 900-g (2-lb) weight on it. Chill for several hours.

4

To serve, turn the pudding out of the basin, spoon the juice over and serve with pouring cream.

Serves 6

Apple-berry fool

WHISK
PLASTIC BLADE

2 eating apples
lemon juice
450 g (1 lb) raspberries, hulled
45 ml (3 level tbsp) sugar
15 ml (1 level tbsp) custard powder
150 ml (¼ pint) milk
150 ml (5 fl oz) double cream
whipped cream to decorate

1

Cut 4 thin slices of apple for decoration and sprinkle with lemon juice to prevent browning. Reserve 4 whole raspberries for decoration.

2

Peel, core and roughly chop the remaining apples and place them in a pan with the raspberries and sugar. Cook gently to a pulp then sieve to remove the pips.

3

Blend the custard powder with a little milk and put the rest of the milk on to heat. Pour the hot milk on to the custard powder blend, stirring, then return it to the pan and stir over gentle heat until thick. Allow to cool a little.

4

Fit the whisk and whip the cream until floppy. Change to the plastic blade and add the fruit mixture. Mix on slow speed until well blended then spoon into glasses and chill.

5

Decorate each glass with a spoonful of whipped cream, an apple slice and a raspberry.

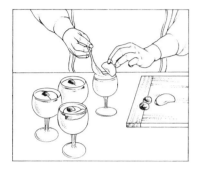

Serves 4

Profiteroles

PLASTIC BLADE

50 g (2 oz) butter or block margarine
about 150 ml ($\frac{1}{4}$ pint) water
65 g (2$\frac{1}{2}$ oz) plain flour, sifted
2 eggs, lightly beaten
150 ml (5 fl oz) double cream
icing sugar to dust

For the chocolate sauce
100 g (4 oz) plain chocolate
170-g (6-oz) can evaporated milk

1

Melt the fat in the water and bring to the boil; remove from the heat and quickly tip in all the flour at once. Beat with a wooden spoon until the paste is smooth and forms a ball in the centre of the pan. Take care not to over-beat or the mixture will become too fatty. Allow to cool for a minute or two.

2

Fit the plastic blade and turn the paste into the bowl. Switch to medium speed and add the eggs gradually through the feeder tube. Carry on mixing until a sheen is obvious.

3

Using a 1-cm ($\frac{1}{2}$-inch) plain vegetable nozzle, pipe small balls of pastry about the size of a walnut on to wetted baking sheets. Bake in the oven at 200°C (400°F) mark 6 for 15–20 minutes until crisp. Make a hole in the side of each ball and return to the oven for 5 minutes. Allow to cool on a wire rack.

4

Fit the whisk and whip the cream. Fill a piping bag, fitted with a plain nozzle, with the cream and use to fill each profiterole. Dust with icing sugar and pile them into a pyramid on a serving plate.

5

Break the chocolate into a saucepan and melt it over a very low heat. Fit the plastic blade and put the evaporated milk in the bowl. Mixing on high speed, pour in the chocolate through the feeder tube. Pour a little chocolate sauce over the profiteroles and serve the rest separately.

Serves 4

Syrup tart

METAL BLADE

**shortcrust pastry made with
100 g (4 oz) plain flour (see
page 119)**
**75 g (3 oz) fresh white bread,
crusts removed**
**60 ml (6 tbsp) golden syrup
grated rind of $\frac{1}{2}$ lemon**

1

Roll out the pastry and use to line
a shallow 18-cm (7-inch) pie plate.

2

Cut the bread into chunks. Fit the
metal blade and chop it to fine
crumbs. Add the syrup and lemon
rind and mix briefly.

3

Spread the mixture in the pastry
case, keeping the border free.
Make cuts down the border at
2.5-cm (1-inch) intervals and fold
over each strip to form a triangle.
Cook in the oven at 220°C (425°F)
mark 7 for about 20 minutes or
until golden brown. Serve hot or
cold with custard sauce.

Serves 4

Pineapple upside-down pudding

PLASTIC BLADE

**50 g (2 oz) butter or block
margarine**
50 g (2 oz) brown sugar
**411-g (14$\frac{1}{2}$-oz) can pineapple
chunks, drained well**
**6 maraschino cherries,
drained well**
**whipped cream or vanilla ice
cream to serve**

For the cake
225 g (8 oz) self raising flour
**225 g (8 oz) butter, softened, or
soft tub margarine**
225 g (8 oz) caster sugar
4 eggs

1

Grease a 33 × 23 cm (13 × 9 inch)
oblong tin and base line it with
greased greaseproof paper. Put the
butter or margarine in the tin and
place it in the oven at 190°C
(375°F) mark 5. Heat until the fat
has melted.

2

Remove the tin from the oven and
sprinkle the sugar evenly over the
base. Arrange the pineapple
chunks on top to make six flower
shapes and place a maraschino
cherry in the centre of each one.

3

Fit the plastic blade and place the
flour in the bowl. Add the butter
or margarine, sugar and eggs and
mix on maximum speed until light
and fluffy. Stop and scrape down
the bowl once during mixing.

4

Spoon the mixture carefully into
the tin and bake for 30 minutes, or
until well risen, golden and firm to
the touch. Cool in the tin on a
wire rack for a few minutes, then
turn out on to a rack to cool
completely. Serve with whipped
cream or vanilla ice cream.

Serves 6

Index